JOURNEY
TO
JERUSALEM

JOURNEY
TO
JERUSALEM

A Play in Three Acts

By
MAXWELL ANDERSON

ANDERSON HOUSE
Washington, D.C.
1940

NOTE

AMATEUR RIGHTS

GEORGE BANTA PUBLISHING COMPANY, MENASHA, WISCONSIN

Preface

BEFORE I wrote *Journey to Jerusalem* I had come to a realization, along with many others in these bitter years, that there was no answer to Hitler and the rule of force except some kind of faith, faith of men in themselves and in the race of men. A Hitler is only possible in a despairing nation, a nation of men who have lost faith in their dignity and destiny, a nation which has no hope except that of conquest, no aspiration except to climb upon the backs of others. Opposition to Hitler is only possible in a nation which retains or can recapture a belief that there are other values beyond those of the materialist. A materialist has no answer to Hitler. Hitler would not be what he is if he had an answer to himself. He believes, quite simply, that there is no value in this world which cannot be expressed in monetary or scientific symbols. His philosophy is that of Iago, and his attitude toward his fellow men is like that of Iago toward Desdemona and Othello and Roderigo and Cassio. They are gulls, to be managed and swindled and brought to ruin through their illusions and emotions. It was part of Iago's scheme that he would be more ruthless than the simple people about him could suspect or conceive. That is also part of Hitler's method.

But modern society has laid itself wider open to Hitler than Venice was to Iago, because there has been a general drift among us toward a belief in salvation by science and machinery. We have pinned our hopes on civilization and progress by material change; we have put aside the ancient wisdom of the race as expressed by the prophets and poets, and have thought, when we did not go so far as to say it, that there is no necessity for a morality based in religion. When a man has admitted that, he is Hitler's meat. If science is to take the place of religion and our morals are to be deduced from science, then the Hitler formula holds: Might makes right, those who are best organized and most ruthless should win, pity and humility and the contrite heart have lost all validity.

For if there are no values beyond scientific values a man is an animal, to be worked, a woman is an animal, to be bred, a child is an animal, to be saved or not according to its usefulness in the practical and piratical scheme of things. The only sources of human dignity and respect for the individual are the great arts, such as poetry, and the great religions, such as Christianity. These are the only bulwarks the race has ever had against despair. Without them we look out on a cold and bleak universe, a complex of revolving forces throughout the sky, a complex of revolving forces within matter, and ourselves here among these forces, quite meaningless to ourselves or to the universe, with no destiny except to eat our quota of meals, sleep our quota of nights, and die meaninglessly at the end of them. This is despair. This is the despair of Hitler and the German people who follow him. Once accepted it leads inevitably to Iago's Machiavellianism, to the glorification of the state, and to mass murder.

If we are to oppose Hitler we must believe in ourselves, as individuals and as a nation. And if we are to believe in ourselves we must—and there is no way out of it— believe that there is purpose and pattern in the universe, that man can contribute to this purpose and that every individual man has a sacred right to follow his own intuition toward that purpose in so far as his actions are compatible with the liberty and happiness of his neighbors. It should be every man's right and privilege to choose his own faith or work it out from his own flashes of revelation. But faith we must have.

It was reflection along these lines that took me back to a study of the origin of Christianity. Weakened though it has been of late years, Christianity is still the strongest influence among us toward that individual dignity upon which individual freedom is established. I have never been a professing Christian, yet I have always found in the teachings of Jesus the most convincing evidence of what we are accustomed to call inspiration. The words of the Sermon on the Mount seem to cut across the dark sky of Palestine under the Caesars like God's own levin flash, lighting up centuries past and centuries to come. There were many great prophets among the Jews, and their words are still impressive. There have been great prophets and seers in the Occident since that time, but I know of no other poem, book, play, passage or sermon which compresses so much dynamic and shattering wisdom into words. My own faith is that these poised, unhurried words come out of depths of meaning which the scientist cannot plumb, and that these words and others from the same depths will, in their own way and time, annihilate Hitler and all Hitlers by teaching men faith in themselves and in their destiny.

It was a study of the Sermon on the Mount in its relation to the old prophets and its own time that tempted me to set down my version of the mystery of the emergence of Jesus. He came out of the ancient Jewish culture, out of a profound study of the great voices of His race, at a time when despair and unfaith had gripped His own people, when the Roman Empire, ruled by sensualists and materialists, hung over a world of doubting and cynical slave-states. He came at a time much like our own in many ways, only further gone into the abyss of despair and surrender. I wanted modern men and women, sitting in an audience, to grasp the problem of unfaith as it presented itself to Jesus when He pondered the Old Testament in His youth, and by what seemed to me a happy chance I came upon the passage in Luke which describes His visit to the temple at twelve years old. This story of the Child of God in the court of the Sanhedrin, finding His way to the meaning of the universe as He walks alone among the columns—this appeared to me the perfect symbol of the soul of man searching for its own meaning. I still think the symbol perfect. My telling of the story is not perfect, I know, but it was written with reverence and with "a bowed mind." If my version of this haunting episode from the New Testament should offend anyone I am truly sorry, but I know that the moving figure of Jesus is too bright and eternal to be shadowed even for a moment, or take any injury, by reason of comment or re-telling.

Notes Concerning the Background
of the Play

ظ ظ

ONE of the strangest facts about the life of Jesus is that
the years between the beginning and the end of His life
are left almost a blank in the New Testament biogra-
phies. His birth and the flight into Egypt are recorded
fully, and His last year and the death are covered with
relative completeness, but of all the weeks between we
have record of only one—the Passover week when He was
twelve years old and went with His family up to Jerusalem to celebrate the annual feast. Luke alone tells this
story, and tells it in his usual beautiful way. It is to him
alone that we owe the picture of the child Jesus as He
stands before the men of the Sanhedrin and answers
their questions with the disconcerting frankness of a
gifted child. Without following Luke's narrative strictly,
Journey to Jerusalem is an attempt to tell the story of
this Passover pilgrimage to Jerusalem and to take the
child Jesus to the threshold of His mission as He walks
alone through the corridors of the temple.

ظ ظ

During the life of Jesus many languages were spoken
along the eastern coast of the Mediterranean. Greek was
still the language of diplomacy and culture; Latin was
the speech of the Roman soldiers, tax-gatherers and offi-
cials who governed the region for the Caesars; Hebrew
was spoken among the priests of the temple at Jerusalem
and taught in the religious schools of the Jews; but Aramaic was the common speech, known to all, and heard
at every market place and street corner. Aramaic was the

speech of Jesus Himself, and when He stood as a child in the Sanhedrin and conversed with the judges, His native dialect and Galilean accent may easily have caused some smiling among the learned men.

ᛞ   ᛞ

According to the historians, Jesus was probably born in 4 B.C. The birth of Jesus was made a starting point in chronology by the monk Dionysius Exiguus, who lived in the sixth century A.D. Before that time, the events and years of the occidental world had been calculated in relation to the founding of Rome or the first Olympic games held in Greece. But these reckonings were inexact and conflicting, and it was not until modern research had combed the records that the facts of ancient history began to assume an exact chronological order. Partly as a consequence of these vague records, an error was made by Exiguus in the date of the birth of Jesus, and the dating of the Christian era was therefore dislocated by four or five years. It follows that Jesus was twelve years old in the year which is known to us as 8 A.D.

ᛞ   ᛞ

Although the revolution of Judah is not mentioned in the New Testament, it was unquestionably the most important public event that took place in Galilee or Judea during the childhood of Jesus. It was a desperate and almost successful revolution against the authority of the Roman governor who had been set over the tribes of Israel after their conquest by Rome. It was suppressed as mercilessly as Hitler has suppressed the resistance of Poland, with thousands crucified and thousands driven into the hills. In those days the mountains along the coast north of Jerusalem were full of bandits and zealots, bands of robbers and companies of holy men who merged with one another, and were often indistinguishable. It is

ᛞ x ᛞ

probable that the evangelism of John the Baptist was a flame still smouldering after the conflagration of Judah's revolt. Throughout the New Testament there are many allusions to this underground life of rebellion which seethed under the iron discipline enforced by Rome through the tetrarch of Galilee, Herod Antipas, and the Procurator of Judea, Pontius Pilate.

ᖬ   ᖬ

The two Herods who touched the life of Jesus are often confused with each other. It was Herod the Great who ordered the death of the children born in 4 B.C. in order to cut off the Messiah in his cradle. It was Herod Antipas, a son of Herod the Great, who, thirty years later, turned Jesus over to the procurator Pilate for execution. Both these Herods derived their power from Rome, for the whole of what is now Palestine had become a Roman province sixty-three years before the birth of Jesus. According to their usual plan, the Roman conquerors had left native rulers behind them to manage these new and recalcitrant subjects. The Herods were part Jewish, part Idumaean in origin, and as the years passed they drifted further from their racial allegiance, tending to imitate the Romans in dress, customs and speech. Herod Antipas would have been mistaken for a Roman in any social gathering.

JOURNEY TO JERUSALEM had its first performance on any stage, in the National Theatre, New York, on Saturday, October 12, 1940, when the drama was produced by the Playwrights Co., Inc., with the following cast in order of appearance.

MARIUS	Arthur L. Sachs
THE GREEK WOMAN	Fay Baker
HEROD	Frederic Tozere
THE SOOTHSAYER	Joseph V. De Santis
MIRA	Alice Reinhert
JOSEPH	Horace Braham
JACOB	Ronny Liss
MIRIAM	Arlene Francis
JESHUA	Sidney Lumet
THE BEGGAR	Joseph Wiseman
SHADRACH	Charles De Sheim
CASSIA	Terry Harris
REBA	Jeannette Chinley
JESSE	Edwin Vail
ZEBULON	Alan Manson
THE CENTURION	Karl Malden
ISHMAEL	Arnold Moss
THE ROBBER	Paul Genge
THE SCRIBE	Henry Lascoe
THE PORTER	Walter Kapp
GENNESARETH	David Leonard
MALACHI	Joseph Kramm
ABBAS	Charles Ellis
CHORAZIM	George Fairchild
HANAN	Byron McGrath
THE DOVE WOMAN	Juliet Talbot
THE 1ST MONEY CHANGER	Arnon Ben-Ami
THE 2ND MONEY CHANGER	Joseph Wiseman
THE PHARISEE	Henry Walden
THE FRUIT SELLER	Joseph Blanton
THE MATZOH SELLER	Katherine Cody
FLACCUS	Paul Genge
FESTUS	James Gregory

JOURNEY TO JERUSALEM
ACT ONE

Act One

Scene I

SCENE ♄ ♄ Before the Temple at Jerusalem, in the year 8 A.D. It is night, and we see only half of one vast column of the Temple, which ascends at the right. At its base are two or three steps leading into the Temple. At the extreme left there is a low wall which marks the boundary of a courtyard before the Temple. A Roman SOLDIER is pacing back and forth between the steps and the wall, looking out occasionally, toward the sky. A WOMAN, wearing a Greek cloak and head-dress, appears at the left.

The Woman. Soldier!

Marius. Yes, woman!

The Woman. I brought the wine.

Marius. You're late.

The Woman. No, soldier; you told me to come
when the red star touched the earth.

Marius. You probably waited
for the wrong star. Or your husband was awake
and you couldn't leave. They say never trust a Greek
or a woman, and you're both.

The Woman. I came when I could.

Marius. Let me have the wine.

> [*She brings out an earthen wine bottle, and a handful of dates.*]

I've been watching those stars go by
six deadly hours, without one human squeak
or rustle to keep me awake. This Jerusalem—

♄ 3 ♄

the Jews must have a good conscience; when they sleep,
by Jupiter, they sleep!

[*He drinks from the bottle.*]

The Woman. And you sleep a little,
just a little sometimes!

Marius. If they caught me asleep here
they'd run a short sword through my lower intestines
and shove me in a corner. No, I don't sleep.
I walk up and down on this sentry path,
and by the procreative gods of Rome,
and the polluted gods of Greece, and the pimping gods
of Egypt, I keep good watch.

[*He eats.*]

The Woman. But here in the night,
by a Jewish temple, where nobody comes
and nobody cares who comes, why should it matter
if it's not guarded?

[*He sits warily, looking about.*]

Marius. Because the king of the Jews
is crazy, my mouse. Herod's crazy, like his father.
He sits there in his palace, and thinks he sees
the walls cracking, and fire leaking up through the
floors,
and devils tearing the curtains. He jumps and glares
and there's nothing there. He thinks the Messiah's
coming
and he'll be snatched down into some Jewish hell
to squirm on a grill—while the Messiah rules
the chosen people. Now Caesar knows Herod's crazy,
and can't trust any Jew to knife the Messiah

when he appears, so Caesar lends a few Romans
to guard key points and satisfy the old dolt
that everything's under control.

The Woman. But this Messiah,
what is he?

Marius. Mouse, I never saw a Messiah,
but I gather he's a kind of Jewish god
from the machine, let down from the Jewish heaven
in a golden chariot of fire, to purge
the heathen. And according to the Jews
you're a Greek heathen and I'm a Roman heathen,
and we ought to be purged. So have a drink.
   [*She takes the bottle. He starts up suddenly to look about.*]

The Woman. Any chariots?
Or gods falling in fire?

Marius. The centurion sometimes
passes this way to check on me. I thought
I heard the jingle of iron.

The Woman. There's no one.

Marius. And twice
Herod Antipas has been here in the night—
in a quilted gown and straw sandals, slopping along
like a market-woman. I knew his yellow face
from seeing it on his shekels.

The Woman. He's in Galilee.
You wouldn't see Herod here.

Marius. Oh, he comes down
to spend a night in Jerusalem, and watch
the procurator and myself. He's serious

about this game of "Look, here comes the Messiah!"
I've been posted
three different places watching for that mule's egg
of his to hatch. I stood guard for three months
on the road from Egypt—then for half a year
I stayed awake nights pacing back and forth across
an alley in Bethlehem.—He shifts the guards
without warning. And no matter where you're stationed
you're likely to see him, shuffling by in the dark,
alone always, and peering back as he goes
to make sure you're there.

The Woman.
   [*Rising*]
What are you supposed to do
if you catch a Messiah?

Marius. Well, an intelligent soldier
destroys the enemy upon contact; I'm
an intelligent soldier—you follow me?

The Woman. But suppose
he comes from the sky with an army?

Marius. Well, who wants to suppose
a thing like that? Look, the last light's gone out
in the governor's palace. The Sadducees and the robbers
and the kings are all in bed beside their women.
Sit here a minute.
   [*They sit down together.*]

The Woman. Wait! I think I heard—
I thought there was something.
   [*She rises, points out left, and runs into the Temple at the
right.* MARIUS *rises, looks out left, and resumes his pacing.*

Not till after he has walked to the left wall and turned, and has come half-way back, does HEROD ANTIPAS *slip out of the shadow at the left and stand watching him.* HEROD *is a middle-aged man, wearing gown and slippers, and some kind of skull-cap for sleeping. He stands staring at* MARIUS, *who turns at the Temple steps and sees him. For a space they are motionless, then* HEROD *turns slowly and goes out.* MARIUS *stands transfixed. The* WOMAN *emerges from the Temple.*]

Marius.

   [*Not turning*]

Stay where you were! Go in!
We came within a hand's-breadth of it, mouse.
They say he burns them hollow with a hot iron
when he catches them with women. Go in, and be quiet.
He's climbing down the path.

CURTAIN

Act One

Scene II

SCENE & & The roof of the palace of Herod Antipas *in Tiberias, Galilee. It is surrounded by low white walls, and looks out over the sleeping city. It is night.* Herod *sits on the wall at the rear, and a* Soothsayer *is seated on the roof, facing him.*

The Soothsayer. It is now understood that each man has
his star, and as this star moves in the heavens
so will the man's life prosper. By his birth in time
his star is known, by the water drop that falls
when the midwife takes his head in her two hands
and brings him forth to earth.

Herod. My star is known?

The Soothsayer. To me only.

Herod. Tell me which is mine.

The Soothsayer. Just before daybreak
it rises over the lake. At this time of year
dawn is your best hour.

Herod. I shall remember that.
Go on.

The Soothsayer. But first, your Highness, is there any truth
you would not wish to hear?

Herod. What kind of truth?

The Soothsayer. The length of life, the threat of evil fortune
to be avoided—

Herod. If it can be avoided
    tell me then. Yes, tell me all of it.
    Only if it should be my death comes soon—
    spare me that.

The Soothsayer. You will outlive your brothers
    and they will all die old.

Herod. I shall outlive them,
    and they shall die old. Yes?
        [MIRA, *the first wife of* HEROD, *enters silently, and stands*
        looking off to the right.]

The Soothsayer. Your star has been
    attacked, and will be attacked again. A comet
    returning every twelve years, fights against
    your star, attempts to shatter it, to dull it,
    to drag it from its course. It was this comet
    that burned over Bethlehem twelve years ago
    and triumphed over your star a single night;
    but that ended well, your father executing
    the children born that year in Bethlehem,
    who would have endangered you. But now the twelfth
      year
    comes round again. The comet will return
    and you must beware.

Herod. Beware of what?

The Soothsayer. Whatever
    threatened you then, threatens you now again.

Herod. The star of the Messiah.

The Soothsayer. It may have been.
    I know nothing of that.

Herod. But if my father
slew the Messiah, among those born that year
in Bethlehem—then there is no Messiah—
and what meaning has the meteor?

The Soothsayer. I can only say
that if an adverse star returns to plague
your guardian fire, then the evil was not killed
but only countered—somehow warded off
or frightened underground.

Herod. If the star return.

The Soothsayer. And it may not appear. For three nights
now
I've stared at the Constellation of the Serpent
all night long, awaiting. It may be
it will not return, for by my own reckoning
it should have come and gone.

Herod. How would you know it?

The Soothsayer. Oh, it would brighten the sky like a
chandelier
let down among candles—

Herod. He would be twelve years old
if he were still alive. His age and birthplace
are identifying marks that could be used
in case a search was made. If this one is not found
then perhaps all should die. Your pardon, Mira,
but if these are your Arab manners, you may keep them
for your return to the desert! This, as you know,
is my hour alone!

Mira. Are you alone?

Herod. Leave us, Mira!
  I have no wish to be angry!

Mira. Your saintly father,
  Herod the Great, made a great slaughter of children,
  a slaughter of the innocents, and made his name
  a horror among men, because he believed
  in some fantastic prophecy concerning
  the birth of this Messiah.

Herod. I know this.

Mira. And remember it?

Herod. Yes. I hold it in my mind
  always—to take no step that will not look sane
  to others—to you, to myself, to anyone
  looking up from among the people, or from abroad,
  from Rome or Egypt. I shall give no order
  that might remind them of my father.

Mira. No?
  What do you contemplate?

Herod. This is the year of the census.
  From every part of Israel and Judea
  the tribes go up to Jerusalem in spring
  to attend the Passover. Once in so many years
  we set our enumerators at the gates
  and make our count for the tax rolls. It will be easy
  to make a special search among the children
  for the one who is prophesied.

Mira. But this prophecy
  and your fear of it, and what action you may take
  to find out the Messiah—these are all
  irrational—

Herod. You are not of our race; you come
   from the desert—

Mira. And I see you as you are!

Herod. I must find a way to make sure I'm not en-
         dangered
      by a Messianic revolution! At present
      I am in danger! There's a star crosses mine!

Mira. A star!

Herod. And not only a star! There's a wind rising—
      and if it storms as it may there'll be little left
      for any son of ours.

Mira. But how are we threatened?
      We're at peace with the world.

Herod. When a man's a ruler
      he feels the tides and currents under him
      as a helmsman feels the sea. I keep a lookout.—
      The revolution of Judah washed clear up
      to the palace walls. The next wave may run higher.
      And what do the agitators cry, and the people
      whisper, like a wind blowing close to the earth?
      Listen and you can hear it—"The Messiah, the Mes-
         siah!"
      You hear it in the back streets, in the shops, among men
      employed to dig the foundations of our palace
      here in Tiberias. It happens the palace site
      was pitched where an ancient Jewish cemetery
      had filled the ground with bones. And the workmen,
         piling
      the bones together, have a saying among themselves,
      "When the Messiah comes these bones will rise
      and tear Herod's palace down!"

Mira. Then what you fear
is only the Messiah!

Herod. I fear him only!
Whatever else God sends a man can meet
and face it like a king! But this seed of fire
that slumbers among the old books, this will breed a
   kingship
that I cannot face and have no weapon for!
I must take him while he is young!
Before he knows his mission, before the people
begin to turn to him! If ten thousand die,
if half my people die, and he die with them,
then I swear it's well done!

Mira. Do you remember
how once you woke me in the night to ask
that if ever I saw signs of the old brain-sickness
your father died of, I should save you from it—
shriek it out at you—have you beaten with whips,
chill you with ice and burn you with fire, but somehow
for our old love keep you sane—?

Herod. Yes, I remember—

Mira. But now it's upon you—this dread of the Messiah
surrounds you like a dream—you never see me—
see no one—see only maniacs—
you will bring us all down together if you persist
in this delusion!

   [HEROD *turns to go, then comes back to her.*]

Herod. Is it in my mind?
It cannot be all in my mind.

Mira. Yes, but it is!

Herod. That would be loathsome. To be like my father,
   To be as he was. And be watched—and know—
   and suspect that you're mad—and wonder—

Mira. Do you know what they say
   about you in the palm-courts and the baths,
   sunning themselves on a Sabbath afternoon,
   and looking about lest someone hear? They say
   he'll die as his father died, choking in the blood
   of children—they say Antipater's gone mad
   with his father's madness—that you see the Messiah
     rising
   out of the very steam of your morning bath,
   and scream for your attendants! They say you search,
   as your father searched, for tokens and entrail-signs
   of this mythical Messiah who will descend
   to overthrow you—till the soldiers scoff in the barracks,
   and Caesar's weary of you—till Caesar says,
   "Humor the madman. The Messianic worm
   kills quickly. Let him alone!" And you are alone
   here with your seers and prophets, like a madman
   shut up with keepers!

Herod. Oh, God of our fathers,
   reveal your truth to me! Let the heavens speak
   or the voice from your whirlwind!

Mira. It was your misfortune
   to be with your father when he died, I think.
   His flesh was tunneled through with living worms,
   and you saw the bright blood bubbling up in his throat
   from his many murders! It will be my misfortune
   to watch you die as he died!

Herod. Take my hand, Mira,

save me! Keep me from that death!
[*A sudden flooding of light falls round them.*]

The Soothsayer. Your Highness,
look toward the Constellation of the Serpent!

Mira. What is it?
What is this light?

The Soothsayer. The comet has returned.

Herod. Then the Messiah lives, and must be dealt with,
and I was not mad! Send for the praetor! Quick,
I shall give the order before his comet dims,
and before my star has risen!
[*He claps his hands. To* MIRA.]

Fool! Fool of a woman!
It's written in the stars the child still lives!
He must be found—and must die!

CURTAIN

Act One

Scene III

SCENE ৬ ৬ The interior of Joseph's *house at Naza-reth. The entrance is at the left, and at this end of the house a number of carpenters' tools and appliances hang or lie about. At the rear wall a long low carpenters' bench has been set where it can be used for a seat. In the middle of the room, somewhat to the right, a curtain, half-drawn, divides the shop from the sleeping apartment. Just to the right of the curtain sits* Miriam, *weaving at a small hand-loom.* Jeshua, *a boy of twelve, is reading intently in a scroll.* Joseph, *the carpenter, sits astride a hurdle, working with a draw-knife on an oxbow.* Jacob, *a younger boy, is reciting a lesson for him.*

Joseph. Will you say it again? And remember the third
reason has to do with something to eat. Think hard
about that and it should be easier.

Jacob. "Tell me why this night
should differ from all other nights of the year?
On other nights we may eat either leavened bread
or unleavened, but tonight only the unleavened;
on other nights we may eat of whatever herbs
we find. Tonight we eat only bitter herbs.
On other nights—"

    [*He pauses.*]

Why do we always leave
an empty place at Passover?—No, I know
that's not what I'm to say, but why is one place
left empty?

Joseph. That's for Elias, if he should come,
or for an angel, if an angel should come in—

or for the Messiah. Or if none of these should come
then for any stranger.

Jacob. But how would one know Elias
or the angel if he came?

Joseph. We might not know,
and so anyone who enters is asked to sit
at the vacant place.—But you haven't said the third
reason.—

Jacob. "On other nights—"
[*He pauses.*]
Oh, but I know it perfectly well except
for those two herbs—the names of those herbs run
backward
away from my mind—and as fast as I run they run faster
so I never catch them—

Joseph. The time will come, my Jacob,
when we all sit in Jerusalem with your father,
and as the youngest it becomes your turn
to open the Haggadah. Then you'll be sorry
you haven't listened and learned.

Jacob. But I do know it
except for the words that run away!

Miriam. Will you look
at the oven once more, Jeshua, and tell me
if the loaves are brown?

Jeshua. Yes, Mother.

Joseph. Before you go
and while I remember it, here are the silver pieces
for the burnt offering. Each child must carry

his portion of silver up to Jerusalem,
and take care of it, and not lose it, for with that
you must purchase the doves for sacrifice.

[*He gives a coin to* JACOB *and then one to* JESHUA.]

Jacob. I shall care for it. And thank you.

Jeshua. Yes, thank you, father.

[*They start to go out.* JACOB *runs ahead of* JESHUA.]

Jacob.

[*Turning at the door*]

Then came the butcher and killed the ox
that drank the water that quenched the fire,
that burned the stick that beat the dog,
that bit the cat that ate the kid
my father bought for two zuzim!
An only kid! An only kid!
So you can't say I don't know that!

[*He runs out.*]

Jeshua. He'll know the rest, too, tomorrow. But he likes
to tease you a little first.

[*He goes out.*]

Joseph. How many loaves are you baking?

Miriam. Only four to eat on the road. Did I hear you say
there's a great census at Jerusalem
this year?

Joseph. Yes.

Miriam. How is it taken?

Joseph. The last time
there was a row of scribes at the city gate

writing at tables. And as each of us passed by
they took down name and age and place of birth
for the Roman tax rolls.

Miriam. Can you think what to say
when we bring Jeshua to the gate?

Joseph. Well, no,
I can't. It keeps coming back to bother me,
but I never find an answer. It has always seemed
the best thing was the truth.

Miriam. And yet the truth—
if we tell it—isn't it possible a soldier
would take him from us—and we'd never hear
what happened?—and torture ourselves forever, thinking
we might have saved him—wondering which dungeon
of Herod's he might lie in?—or might be dead—
or might be better dead?

Joseph. Yes, yes, I know.

Miriam. In all Bethlehem and round about they say
there are no boys twelve years old. If a lad came down
this spring to Jerusalem, and told the scribes
quite calmly, I was born in Bethlehem,
my age is twelve—

Joseph. Then the scribe would say, without doubt,
this is the child the first Herod overlooked—
this is the child our Herod's hunting for—
this is the budding horn of the Messiah
that must be nipped before it grows too tough
for the Roman pincers.

Miriam. If it be true—what sometimes

we have said—then it may be God cares for him—
and yet—if it be true—perhaps our God
expects of us that we be doubly careful
of what's so precious.

Joseph. Could we speak to him? Could we some way
  prepare him?
Tell him that this is only a doubtful guess—
and yet it may be true—and he must therefore
be wary in his answers?

Miriam. No, truly, Joseph—
Whatever is in him he must find himself—
Whatever he is to be—he must discover—
We must never say it—never until he asks,
I know this
as if I were being warned to let him walk
to the gate without taking thought. Yet if I were wrong,
and he should tell his truth quite innocently,
and never speak again—

Joseph. We shall be three days
on the way to Jerusalem. Some thought may come
before we're at the gate.

> [*An emaciated* BEGGAR, *bent over and with a sack on his
> back, appears in the doorway.*]

The Beggar. You're Joseph of Nazareth?

Joseph. Yes.

Beggar. I won't give my name,
though you might know it. My name wore off me with
the clothes I had when I went into the hills.
I'm one of the few remaining culls left over
from the revolution of Judah. There are thirty of us
still hiding above on Mount Tabor. What we get to eat

I leave you to imagine. We won't trouble you long,
nor anyone. But whatever you have in the house
that you were about to throw away—I'll take it.
A little mould or mildew wouldn't matter,
and we're used to worms in the meal.

Miriam. There's half a loaf
left over from our supper.

The Beggar. If it means you go hungry
never mind it. They'll get us before the year's out,
and whether it's better to starve or rot on a cross
we haven't decided yet.

Joseph. The revolution
is seven years old. Are there still thirty men
at large in the hills?

The Beggar. There are thousands, one place and another.
But the fight's gone out of us. And the fight's lost, too.
The Roman tax is here to stay, and the Romans
are here to stay, at least for our time. And Judah's
dead, and we're dying.
   [*He turns.*]
If it's true about
the half loaf, let me have it.
   [*As* MIRIAM *fetches the bread the two* BOYS *re-enter.*]

Joseph. I only wish
that it were more.

The Beggar. You could give more, but why should you?
You could have fought when we fought, but why should
   you—
because we lost.

Joseph. They rejected me from the phalanx.
I wasn't young enough.

The Beggar. I was young enough.
God knows I'm old enough now. The greeting of God
go with you for the half loaf.
  [*He goes out.*]

Jeshua. What man was that?

Joseph. We're not a free people. Seventy years ago
the Romans came this way, and since that time
their governors have ruled our kings. Our high priests
are appointed from Rome; we pay a tax to Rome
and another to Herod. But it's all Rome. We're not free,
and seven years ago a man named Judah
led a revolt against the Roman census
and the Roman tax. He's dead now, and this man
was one who followed him. Will follow him further,
to the end of what can be done to a man.
  [*They are silent for a moment.*]

Miriam. Are the loaves ready?

Jeshua. Not yet, I think, Mother.
  [*A* VOICE *is heard from beyond the door.*]

The Voice. Some of the most unappetizing people
emerge from this residence.

Joseph. It's Shadrach and the others.
Come in, come in!
  [SHADRACH, *a carpenter, enters with his wife,* CASSIA. *They
  are followed by two stone-masons,* ZEBULON *and* JESSE, *and
  their wives,* REBA *and* ESTHER. SHADRACH *carries a torch,
  which he puts out.*]

Shadrach. There was a cabbage-green
sort of bitten-off fellow, with a sack on his back
that came out of here. Have you missed anything?

Joseph. No, Shadrach,
only a bit of bread.

Shadrach. This part of town
will get a bad name, if it allows gangrene beggars
that smell like that.—Now any other color—
but this squeamish-green!

Miriam. Come in, all of you.

Cassia. And don't mind Shadrach;
he has a good heart.

Shadrach. No, but that was a spoiled man; he was mouldy;
he was on his way back into the substance
from which we don't admit we come—

Miriam. Sit here
and rest, mother Reba. See, Cassia, we have
new rush mats, so that all can sleep here tonight
and start early in the morning. And the blessing of God
on all of you, since Shadrach must break in
without God's blessing.

> [*She smiles at* SHADRACH.]

Reba. God's greeting to the house.

Cassia and Esther. And to all here.

> [*The two* MASONS *mumble a pious word with them.*]

Shadrach. Did I leave that out? The truth is
I've been God's-greeting the wide world today
and I want a place to sit down. The blessing of God
on the house and its accommodations!

> [*He settles himself.*]

Zebulon. We took
to the road before noon.

Joseph. Perhaps you'll be too weary
to start again in the morning.

Zebulon. No, I think not.
We'll make it a three-day journey, and cool our feet
in the river when we're tired.

Jesse. When we were young
Jerusalem was only two days' away
by the path along hither Jordan. Now, of course,
even the young folks take three days to it.

Shadrach. Yes,
and why not? It's our one holiday. I work
every day in the year, except holy days, and so
does Cassia. But then when the spring comes round
I begin to smell the Passover feast. That's once
we can forget about hammers and nails and prices
and set off across country like young lovers. I tell you
I'm no strict believer—
give me Ecclesiastes for my money—
"Vanity of vanities, all is vanity,"
there's a prophet—of the making of many books
and the laying of many bricks, and even the sawing
of many boards, there's no end—

Joseph. You were about
to say something?

Shadrach. Yes, I was! I was about to say
man is of few days, and evil—he's born to trouble
as the sparks fly upward, and wherever he walks
there's a hollow place preparing in the ground
to house him at the last—so let him have

three days on the way to Jerusalem.—It's spring
and the flowers are out in the desert.

Miriam. I'm always grateful
that Passover comes in the spring when the desert lilies
are at their best. There's a kind of happiness
in the temple courts; one's happy just to see
the Sanhedrin, and to know that some men are wise
and care for wisdom—but what one remembers most
is sleeping open to the air, and singing
as we did when we were children, then waking to find
the Jordan suddenly, and turning inland
and returning to find it again.

Joseph. We'll take the three days.

Jesse. Sometimes I wonder about this Ecclesiastes
when he seems to be saying that nothing matters and
   there's
no God, and the life of man is wind. I wonder
about Ecclesiastes.

Cassia. And about Shadrach?
   [*She touches* SHADRACH'S *hair.*]

Jesse. Yes,
about Shadrach, too.

Cassia. Yes, I wonder about him.
For a good husband and a good carpenter
he has some remarkably sharp things to say
about man's evil days.

Shadrach. Few and evil. All too few
to spend with so lovely a woman.
   [*He puts an arm around her.*]

Miriam. I must look at my loaves.
I'm baking for the journey.

Cassia. I'll go with you.

Miriam. And since we start early, perhaps you should
choose your own pallets
where you'll sleep. Mother Reba will have my bed,
if she doesn't mind—

Reba. No, girl—I'm for the floor
with the younger pilgrims.

[MIRIAM, CASSIA *and* ESTHER *go out. A Roman* CENTURION
appears in the entrance.]

The Centurion. This is the house of Joseph the carpenter,
or so I'm told?

Joseph. You wish to see me?

The Centurion.

[*Affably*]

You're a fine set of treasonous heathen, you are, live
down here among rocks and ditches, where a Roman
can't find his way even by daylight. I think you do it
to make soldiers break their necks.

Joseph. We hardly know
there are stones and ditches, we're so used to them.

The Centurion. Well, forget about that. I came on another matter.
You're a carpenter, and now I see you have guests,
and they're carpenters and masons. I'm here about
the palace at Tiberias—Herod's new palace,
and the work on it. When I saw you last at the market
I told you we'd need carpenters and masons

to work there in the spring. Well, now it's spring,
and we haven't seen you. A female devil take
those rocks! They've cut a strap in two!
> [*He works at his sandal.*]

Joseph. As you know
next week is set aside for our festival
and we shall all be in Jerusalem.

The Centurion. I know,
and I have my orders not to interfere
with a Jewish festival. That's understood
between Herod and the governor and whoever else
makes out the edicts. But I'm also told
to damn well get the palace built, and get
the men to do it. And the men aren't there.
And I'm here, as you may have noticed, and my neck's
not broken so far.

Joseph. Is it not understood
also, that a workman may pick and choose
among the tasks that offer, thinking of the wage,
and whether the overseers are of his race,
and the distance from his home?

The Centurion. There's no wage better.
We're authorized to pay the best wage there is.
And as for the overseers, I'll make you one
with your own men under you. You're known around
for an honest man, and we'll trust you.

Joseph. Let me think
and give you an answer.

The Centurion. I won't come again.
Not through your scarps and outworks. Answer me
now.

Will you come when you're through with your Passover?

Shadrach. If you'll forgive me
I think the Centurion should be told the reason
why we avoid Herod's palace, and prefer
not to work on it.

The Centurion. Why?

Joseph. Have you never heard
that Herod's new palace in Tiberias
is built on the oldest Jewish graveyard known
in Galilee? Our fathers were buried there,
yet I've seen the bones of Jewish patriarchs
corded up by the workmen in long rows
out in the sun and rain!

The Centurion. Well, Herod's your man,
not ours!

Joseph. And not ours! He's no Jew, and wouldn't stay
long
where he is without a Roman guard behind him
and Caesar reaching from Rome!

The Centurion. Oh, Mother of Hermes,
are we so touchy about our father's bones?
You'd better take more care of the living skin
that grows on your backs!

[MIRIAM *and* CASSIA *re-enter, carrying four loaves of bread.*]

Stand up and bring your faces nearer the light
so that I'll remember them.

[*The* MEN *stand.*]

You had a helper
when you worked at Capernaum.

Joseph. My son Jeshua.
He acted as my helper.

The Centurion. Let him stand, too.

[JESHUA *ranges himself with the others.*]

When you've had your holiday,
and taken your time about it, as you will,
no doubt, you'll come to work on Herod's palace,
and I'll hold you responsible for the others. Bring
your son.

Joseph. He's still at school.

The Centurion. Bring him anyway.
I'm being tender with you, my dear Joseph.
The only question is—will you say yes
to a pleasant man like me, or must they send
another less pleasant? You'll have to answer now
because I'm short of time.

Joseph. Sir, there are no slaves
in Galilee.

The Centurion. There are ways around that, too.
There are ways. And since it's no skin off my knuckles
I'm going.

[*He turns.*]

Miriam.

[*Desperate*]

The work's done better when it's done gladly.
What good will come of a building if the masons
pour in a curse with the mortar, and the carpenters
peg the beams with curses?

The Centurion. Curses won't hurt.
The empire stands on curses, and I've stept

on a number of cursing mouths myself. No Roman
dies of the evil eye.

Miriam. But let them answer
after the Passover. Maybe some mind will change.
Let us not run after evil. Let us meet it
when it has caught up with us.

The Centurion. You Jews go out
to meet it, and drag it in with you.

[*He sees the loaves.*]

Speaking of bread,
somebody gave half a loaf to one of Judah's
outlaws—a known rebel. We took it from him
and here it is.

[*He pulls a sack from under his arm.*]

Now we know that nobody here
would provision an outlaw, the penalty being death.
Yet he'd been here, and had the bread with him. You
see,
I'm being tender with you.—

[*He lays the sack on the bench.*]

You may as well keep it.
The fellow you gave it to is lying down
where he won't be eating bread.—I'll expect to see you
after Passover—in Tiberias.

[*He goes out.*]

CURTAIN

Act One

SCENE IV

SCENE ♌ ♌ A desert place below Jericho on the west side of the Jordan. A gigantic rock lifts at the right, and under its foot a fire is smouldering. To the left a smaller boulder encloses the scene. It is the second night's encampment on the way to Jerusalem, and those who were planning the journey in the last scene are preparing for the night or already lying on their shawls and blankets. Someone has begun a chant, and all sing together the last chapter of Ecclesiastes:

Remember now thy Creator
in the days of thy youth,
while the evil days come not, nor the years draw nigh
when thou shalt say, "I have no pleasure in them."

While the sun or the light,
or the moon or the stars, be not darkened,
nor the clouds return after the rain.

Or ever the silver cord be loosed
or the golden bowl be broken,
or the pitcher be broken at the fountain,
or the wheel broken at the cistern.

Then shall the dust return to the earth as it was,
and the spirit unto God who gave it.

Cassia.

    [*Rising, looking to the left*]

Shadrach!

Zebulon. There was a shadow moving among the rocks;
he may be taking a look about.

Jesse. Alone?
He should have carried a light.

Zebulon. Surely no wild beast
would come so close to our fire.

Joseph. I'll walk out that way.
I think I hear him.
　[He steps out left.]

Jesse. There were voices along the river
earlier in the evening.
　[By this time a number have risen and look out to the left.]

Jacob. Is it true
there are lions in the desert, Mother?

Miriam. No,
not here, I think. We're only one day's journey
from Jerusalem city. On the other side of the river
there may be lions.

Jacob. And leopards?

Miriam. Yes, leopards, too.

Jacob. Don't you remember in the book of Kings
there were lions this side of the Jordan?

Miriam. Yes, long ago,
there may have been then.

Jacob. I think there are lions here.
　[He sits up.]
I really think so. It's not such a wide river.
They could come right across.

Jeshua. Did I ever tell you the story
of the lion who wouldn't get his feet wet?

Jacob. No.

ひ 32 ひ

Jeshua. Once there was a lion who lived alone
in the trans-Jordan country. He lived quite well
there on the other side of the river, and ate
nearly every day. But then there came a season
when all things failed on his side of the river.

[JACOB *lies back to listen.*]

He couldn't find anything, not even a cony
among the rocks, and so every day he sat empty
and looked across the river at hither-Jordan
and cried because he was hungry, and looked at his
  paws
and licked them, and cried. And he said to himself,
"This hunger
is a terrible thing; it's a thing stronger than lions,
because it's stronger than I am." Then he set one paw
in the shallow of the river, and said, "This water
is an ancient enemy, and I dislike it,
but I must cross the river, and taste the sheep
on the hills of hither-Jordan." Then he shook his paw,
like this, to shake the water from it, and roared,
and put in another foot, and snarled, and said,
"This hunger is stronger than I am, but I am stronger
than water!" and at that he jumped straight in
and beat the river with his paws, and choked,
and jumped out again. Then the lion said. "It seems
I was mistaken. A great lion like myself
is stronger than hunger. I'm not hungry at all."
So he licked himself all over and lay down
and looked very fierce, but the trouble really was
he was afraid of water. And from that day
there are no lions on this side.

Jacob. But didn't he ever
get anything to eat?

Jeshua. Yes, after a while—
in the rainy season. But no matter how hungry he was
he never swam the river.
[JOSEPH *returns from the left.*]

Joseph. He's not that way.
I think he's walked on up the valley.

Cassia.
[*Calling*]
Shadrach!

Esther. Isn't there a fire? I saw the flash of a fire.
[*She looks out to the right.*]

Zebulon. Yes, and that's where he's gone. There's another
encampment
like our own.

Reba. Then what was the need to frighten
the women and children? My legs give way and bend
all the way down, like a pair of tallow candles
in a warm house.

Jesse. Yes, I do see a fire,
and someone coming this way.

Zebulon. This will be Shadrach.
[*There is a moment's pause. They wait silently.*]

Shadrach.
[*Entering from the right*]
We must put out our fire and move our camp
toward the path along the river. Gather your things!
Quick, Cassia! Quick, all of you—and the children—
we'll find another place!

Cassia. But why, Shadrach?

Shadrach. Never mind—
only we move.

Jesse. What have you seen?
[*The company stirs itself to move.*]

Shadrach. It wasn't
so much what I saw as what I heard. A nest
of wild men warming their hands around a fire
and estimating gravely what we're worth
in gold or silver—or hides. I've heard of these naked
and hairy bandits in the hills, but these
are hairier than I expected. Come,
if our fire's out, and we've vanished, they'll give up
and turn on somebody else.

Jacob. Maybe they're lions.

Shadrach. No, they're not lions. They're men, but not
of the sort
I want to talk with.
[*As he speaks, a half-naked emaciated* MAN *with a sword in his hand appears behind him. He turns, and two or three other* BANDITS *enter. Some carry weapons, some staves.*]

Ishmael.
[*The 1st* BANDIT]
You are on your way
to the holy city? 460156

Shadrach. Yes.

Ishmael. How many of you?

Joseph. Ten.

Ishmael. Do you bear offerings?

Joseph. No.

Ishmael. Have you money
to pay for offerings?
  [*They are silent.*]
Answer as if you stood
in the presence of your God, for you are held
responsible in your answers.

Joseph. There is no one here
who knows what the others have. What little we carry
in silver or copper coins we took with us
to buy our sacrifices.

Ishmael. And do you not know
that whatever you buy in the temple courts yields profit
to Hanan the high priest, and that Hanan paid
for his place, giving money to Herod, and Herod in
    turn
bought his seat from Augustus? Is it worship of God
that pays tribute to Rome?

Joseph. Sir, we have heard these things,
or guessed at them indirectly. But a man
must worship God, and his family must worship,
and in all the sacred books there is no door open
for access unto God, save the rites of the temple,
and the high priest of our people. If these be corrupt
are we corrupted, worshipping? And if so,
should we then shut ourselves from God entirely,
and eat as the beast eats, without thought or thanks
for Him who made him?

Ishmael. How can I answer you, you who have forgotten
    Judah?
How can I answer you

who bow your necks to the oxbow and plow for Herod
and reap for Caesar?
Who pour out money for burnt offerings
on a captured altar, and think God is pleased?
You and those with you have betrayed your God,
as, when Judah was dying, you betrayed him,
sending no succor to him!

2nd Robber. The men will come forward
and give over what money they have.

Ishmael. Then if afterward you are searched
and money is found on a man, then by Jehovah
and by our Judah, that man shall die, and be nailed
to the desert floor with thorn-sticks sharpened in fire!

Joseph. Will you tell me your name?

Ishmael. They call me Ishmael
because my hand is raised against every tribe
that sends up tribute to Rome!

Joseph. We must pay them quietly, Shadrach, for these
men
are armed, and we are not.
  [*He detaches a purse from his girdle and surrenders it.*]

Shadrach. Very well.
  [*He also pays, followed by* JESSE *and* ZEBULON.]

Joseph. Were you a follower of Judah?

Ishmael. Yes.

Joseph. And did Judah hold it righteous
to rob pilgrims in the desert?

Ishmael. No, but the days have made it righteous!

Joseph. And are you a prophet,
  to say what is righteous?

Ishmael. Come up into the hills with me,
  you who travel easily to Jerusalem!
  Come into the hills, and I will show you the men
  who followed Judah; how some of them are sick
  and there is no physician,
  how some of them are stricken with the sun
  and some with hunger,
  and some have died of cold, without covering,
  and day and night, when the noon is fire, or the dark-
    ness
  falls like a winter, there are always the Romans, the
    Romans
  out of their camps, with metal shields before them,
  and short swords thrusting at the belly!
  This is our life. And you are soft and have not helped
    us.
  You will help now a little. Against your will.

Joseph. But even if this is true, could I not say,
  "Lo, I am a poor man, and my neighbor is rich;
  I will go to my neighbor and take from him
  lest my child hunger tomorrow?"

Ishmael. Would you hear what Judah said when he was
    dying?
  This was the message of Judah, "The Messiah is born
  who will conquer the Romans!
  His star has been seen, and he lives,
  and he will deliver us!
  Whether he come in fire, with wings of iron,
  or with chariots over the earth,
  whether he come with thousands or alone,

he will deliver Galilee and Judaea!
Therefore wait for the Messiah, and keep watch,
and you who are called Ishmael, keep you my men,
this little remnant, keep them and live in hope;
for the old law has been broken like tablets of glass,
and shall bind you under no more!
And no man ever again shall loose or bind
save the Messiah, who now lives among you,
and has not spoken, but will speak, and burn out
the hearts of over-lords, and wither kingships—
till there's neither procurator nor tax
nor Caesar left above you!" This said Judah
when he was dying, and he died above in the hills
of an old wound. And we wait here for the Messiah,
even robbers, even sleepers in the rain,
but doing the will of God!

Shadrach. It won't help to argue with a madman, Joseph,
and these folks are plainly mad.

Zebulon. Yes, they are mad.

Joseph. Then the Messiah lives?

Ishmael. This too was promised me when he lay dying,
by Judah, that I should see the Messiah, though he
should never see him. Now I am dying too,
for I have a mortal lesion, and can live
but a few days. Yet I shall see him, for this
was prophesied.—But go to Jerusalem!
As the Jordan runs to Bahr Lut—to the Dead Sea,
go down to that sink which is called Jerusalem!
Worship a shame-faced god at his dirtied altar!
Kneel down in the courts where kneeling is at a price,
and harken to Pharisees! But remember, rising,

that you have fed for a day those who kneel among
   rocks,
who worship a free God freely, and await
that which is promised, and will come!
   [He turns to go.]

Jeshua. Ishmael!

Jesse. Be quiet,
   and let him go.

Ishmael. Did someone call me?

Shadrach. No!
   These are insane men, Jeshua, and criminals;
   let them go if they will.

Jeshua. Will you take my silver?

Ishmael. Who was it called me?

Miriam. They have taken enough, Jeshua.
   We shall come penniless to my brother's house.

Jeshua. I should like to give him my silver, Mother.

Shadrach. Well,
   now that they know he has it—
   *[He shrugs and turns away. JESHUA crosses to ISHMAEL and
   offers him the coin.]*

Ishmael. You give this freely?

Jeshua. Yes, freely.

Ishmael. You are not frightened?

Jeshua. No, not frightened.
   But I cannot give it unless you put out your hand—
   and I wish to give it.

Ishmael. What is your name?

Jeshua. Jeshua.

Ishmael. And how old are you?

Jeshua. Twelve.

Ishmael. And where were you born?

Jeshua. In Bethlehem.
  [ISHMAEL *takes the silver.*]

Ishmael. Let me see your face.
  Now blessed be the God
  of Judah, who has let me live to this hour.—
  Give back what we have taken,
  for this is a holy company. And go quickly
  into the hills, and bring news there we are gone
  to Jerusalem—for our waiting nears an end,
  and those who live shall have sight of him!
    [*The 2nd* ROBBER *restores the money to* JOSEPH, *and goes
    out.*]
  Lie down
  and rest, and we will guard you. Yes, many more
  will come from the hills to guard you. I keep only
  this silver penny, as earnest of the kingdom.

Jeshua.
    [*Coming down to his* FATHER *and* MOTHER]
  Why does he look at me?

Shadrach
    [*Tapping his forehead*]
  He's touched. They're all touched,
  But they have their uses.

Joseph. There was some kind of magic
in your gift of silver.

Miriam. It's not a usual thing
that they receive alms.

Zebulon. What does this mean to you?

Jesse. I gather one thing:
They've given the money back.

Shadrach. And they're setting a guard.

Zebulon. But these are robbers
and desperate men. Do we dare lie down and close
our eyes and let them guard us?

Shadrach. I shall lie down,
because I'm tired. Besides, what else can we do?

Jesse. Well, sleep well, Shadrach.

Shadrach. Oh, I shall sleep well. I always sleep my sound-
est guarded by robbers.

CURTAIN

Act One

Scene V

*SCENE ♄ ♄ Evening before the city gates of Jerusalem.
A SCRIBE sits writing at a small table; a line of people is
forming to the right. The party that we know has arrived
and is now answering. MARIUS, who has been posted at the
gate, approaches to listen. JESHUA has perched on a rock
at the rear, and reads a scroll. A WOMAN passes the group
and enters the gates. She carries bird cages on her back.*

The Dove Seller. Buy my pigeons and doves! Buy my white
doves!

Buy my pigeons and doves! Buy my white doves!

The Scribe.

   [*To* REBA]

Your birthplace?

Reba. Capernaum.

The Scribe. Your age?

Reba. Sixty-five.

   [*He nods to her. She passes on.* JESSE *comes next to the
   table.* MIRIAM *and* JOSEPH *sit on a stone a little forward
   from the others.*]

Joseph. The soldier has come out from the gate.

Miriam. Yes. He listens.

Oh, Joseph—have we trusted too much? My breath
fails me—

and my heart. Shall we go back? Shall we turn

and not stay for the Passover?

Joseph. But all eyes would be upon us—

and those who thought no harm of us might then
wonder

why we had been afraid.

The Scribe.
[*Angry*]
Must you mumble your words
down toward the earth?

Jesse. Sir?

The Scribe.
[*To* MARIUS]
God pity the census-taker.
Humanity poured over him like a vomit;
the infirmity of age, the noses and rears
of inarticulate children, the—

Marius. It's a long day
here from sun-up to sun-down and your pen
gets worn down like your patience—

The Scribe. Well, pass on.
I think I have it.

Marius. The porter's coming now
to close the gates.

The Scribe. Jesse, the son of Kerith,
living in Nazareth, sixty-nine years old,
a mason.

Jesse. Yes, sir.

The Scribe.
[*Looking at* JACOB, *who is in line behind* JESSE.]
Is this your son?

Jesse. Why, no, sir.

The Scribe. Your grandson?

Jesse. No, sir.

The Scribe. Are you his guardian?

Jesse. No.

The Scribe. Then why does he come pushing in behind
you?
Who's with you?

Jacob. I can answer for myself.
I'm Jacob, the son of the judge, Gennesareth,
I was born in Jerusalem, and I live there; see—
I'm here with my kinsman Joseph.

Marius. Ask his age.

The Scribe. Your age?

Jacob. Ten years old.

The Scribe.
   [*To* JOSEPH]
   This boy is with you?

Joseph. Yes.

The Scribe. These answers are correct?

Joseph. Yes. Quite correct.

The Scribe. Pass in, then. And hurry. The sun has touched
the hill,
thank God, and the gates will soon be closing. Come,
your name?
   [SHADRACH *steps before the table.* JESHUA *continues to read
   obliviously.*]

Shadrach. Shadrach of Nazareth, a carpenter.

Joseph. We can't leave now.

Miriam. No.

Joseph. The soldier
wished to know Jacob's age. It would have been better
to hide in Egypt—or sleep in a cave of the mountains
out toward Phoenicia. To have kept no feasts, and
lived only to guard him from them.

Miriam. Let us leave now, Joseph.
Jacob will enter the city with the others,
but you and I and Jeshua must turn back.
and find our way home. I feel it strongly—we must—
no matter what may be said—

Joseph. Yes, I feel it strongly—
and yet I ask too why there's been no sign
if there was danger.

Miriam. We are lost now if we pause!
Come, we will turn together, and, if they call,
we will not enter still, but give quite different names
and be seen no more at Nazareth, be seen
no more in any city—

Joseph, I fear even that
may be fatal now. They look at us under brows
and wait for us—
> [*They turn to take their places before the* SCRIBE. *At this
> moment* ISHMAEL *and the* 2nd ROBBER *enter and take their
> places at the table where Joseph and Miriam would have
> stood.*]

The Scribe. Speak then. Your name?

Ishmael. Ishmael.

The Scribe. And occupation?

Ishmael. I gather desert honey, and parch grain over the
fire, and study God's word.

The Scribe. That's three occupations. And none recog-
nized.
Will you give me one that I can write down here
as a livelihood among civilized men?

Ishmael. I will.—
I study God's word.

The Scribe. And are you paid for that?

Ishmael. I'm paid in the words
of God, and in understanding of His words.
Are any paid better?

The Scribe.
[*Looking up at him, then smothering his anger*]
Let it go. Where do you live?

Ishmael. In Bethábara, in the desert of the Salt Sea.
I have my brother with me, and my son.
My brother, who stands behind me, is deaf and dumb,
and cannot speak for himself. His name is Dark,
and we are the sons of Rabbath.
[*The* SCRIBE *writes.*]

The Scribe. And your own son,
do you have him with you?

Ishmael. Yonder, reading the scroll,
the lad there yonder.
[JESHUA *looks up and listens.*]

The Scribe. And his name?

Ishmael. Jeshua.

The Scribe. And where was he born?

Ishmael. Sir, on the slopes of Mount Nebo where his
    mother
was tending flock. In no city and no town
but desert born.

Marius Who has taught him to read?

Ishmael. I taught him to read.
He reads the word of God.

The Scribe. What is his age?

Ishmael. He is thirteen years old.
> [JESHUA *gets down and crosses to* MIRIAM, *who puts her finger to her lips.*]

Miriam. Say nothing, and go with him.

The Scribe. And now if you'll kindly pull all your wits
    together in an effort to make sense, we'll have a last try
    at your occupation. Something must be set down
as the thing you do.—

Ishmael. I have told you I gather honey
and parch corn over the fire, and study God's word!

The Scribe. Are you paid for any of these?

Ishmael. I am not paid.

The Scribe. But when you need money for taxes, and all
    men born
pay taxes, where do you get it?

Ishmael. You may set down
  that I sell the honey.

The Scribe. Well, I will set it down,
  but the desert north of Nebo is full of robbers
  and I have no doubt you're among them, both of you,
  if the truth were known.

Ishmael. And Jerusalem, your city,
  is full of robbers, and that truth is known,
  full of scribes and Levites and Pharisees
  and Sadducees, sucking the very gristle
  from children's bones, to make profit of gold and silver
  for Herod and his Arabian wife!

The Scribe. Very well—
  but I say you're a robber, as most of them are robbers
  across the Jordan, and ripe for crucifixion,
  and they'll get you before you're through!

Ishmael. But first the scribes
  and Levites—and the ravenous house of Hanan—
  God will see them hung up first!

The Scribe. As you like. Go in
  before they shut the gates.
    [*To* JESHUA]
  Go in with your father.
    [JESHUA *follows Ishmael.*]
  Jeshua!

Jeshua. Yes?

The Scribe. That is your name? Jeshua?

Jeshua. Yes.

The Scribe. What is it you read?

Jeshua. This scroll?
The book of Isaiah.
Only these latter chapters of Isaiah
were written by an Unknown Prophet, of whom the name
even has been lost.

The Scribe. And what does it say in the book?

Jeshau. Here where I read it says that the earth was better
at one time, and will be again.

The Scribe. Do you believe that?

Jeshua. Yes, I believe it.

The Scribe. Go in.

    [JESHUA *goes in.* JOSEPH *and* MIRIAM *come to the table.*]

The Scribe, Yes?

Joseph. Joseph of Nazareth,
a carpenter, and his wife Miriam.

The Scribe. There's a boy with you
named Jacob, who went in before you?

Joseph. Yes.

The Scribe.

    [*Writing*]

Go in then. The porter may close the gates. The sun
went down some time ago.

    [JOSEPH *and* MIRIAM *go inside. The* PORTER *begins to shut
the gates.*]

Marius. We shall have the old fox Herod
here tomorrow, and we've caught nothing yet.

The Scribe. No.

Marius. This last lad—you called him to make him turn—
for a look at his face?

The Scribe. To make him answer his name—
and say what he was reading.

Marius. He was reading Isaiah,
Whatever Isaiah is.

The Scribe. It's a holy book. Quite holy enough
to make him the madman's son.

Marius.
  [*To the* PORTER]
Let us through before it's locked, boy. Wait, let us
  through.
We're too old to pile over it.
  [*They go in.*]

CURTAIN

JOURNEY TO JERUSALEM

ACT TWO

Act Two

Scene I

SCENE & & An inner room of the Temple, used for the meetings of the Sanhedrin. The session is over for the day, but a few members linger to discuss an unfinished question.

Gennesareth. We are all friends of the high priest—or must seem
  to be his friends. Our seats in the Sanhedrin
  would soon be filled with others if we dared
  dispute his policy. But when you have walked
  through the streets of Jerusalem, have you turned suddenly
  by chance and seen the curious eyes upon you
  there in the crowd? Eyes that say, "This is a priest,
  and I should reverence him," but which also say,
  "This man serves under Hanan, and Hanan serves
  under Herod, and all three stand together between
  my God and me. How can reverence to them
  be reverence to my God?" You have seen this question
  in people's eyes—and you have wondered, too,
  "Do we serve God or do we serve corruption,
  here in the temple?"

Malachi. Only people who are free
  may serve God as they please.

Gennesareth. Then when will our day
  of deliverance come? How long will our God be kept
  a prisoner at His own altar—and we His jailors,
  paid to betray Him in Silence?

Abbas. A visitor.

The high priest Hanan.
[HANAN *enters.*]

Hanan. Forgive me, gentlemen. I asked you to wait
after the others were gone, because I have
a peculiar message for you from our Lord Herod,
a message and a commission. You are men of the spirit
and he of the flesh—or such is his word to you—
and there are matters wherein he is blind
though you may be able to see. Among these matters
is that of the Messiah's coming. This
has been foretold by seers you study hourly,
and when this prophecy has come to pass
it will be those attuned to it in mind
who will first know—who will feel the first faint trem-
bling
of earth beneath the footstep of its king
and be aware of him. And your commission
from Herod is only this—when you first know
or first suspect his presence in our midst—
it is his wish that you will send this news
through me to him. Or directly if you will.
For Herod and myself wish to do him honor
and submit ourselves to his kingdom.—I come to ask
for Herod—as from himself—if this magic news
should touch you, will you come first to us, that we
may share your happiness?

Abbas. If it comes to us
you shall hear, lord Hanan.

Ghorazim. And if this revelation
should come to you, a much more likely thing,
you being the high priest and the friend of God,
will you not share it with us then, so that we
may worship with you?

Hanan. You have my word for that, if God should favor
   me.

Chorazim. Thank you, my lord.

Hanan. Also—I hope you have not mistaken Herod—
   he is a mystic and a dreamer of dreams,
   but his dreams are the same as yours. Until tomorrow.
   [*He goes out.*]

Chorazim. Yes, my lord.

Gennesareth. The adder in the nest!
   A snake could argue quite as plausibly
   that he means to worship the bird!

Abbas. But do you think so?

Gennesareth. This welcome prepared—

Abbas. Yes—?

Gennesareth. Is a quiet murder.
   And what he asks is that we join with him
   in a conspiracy to destroy the Messiah!

Malachi. Come!
   Come, sir, the head of our church does not conspire
   with the head of our state against what might be called
   the flowering of our race. They and all of us
   would gain by that flowering.

Chorazim. You refer, I believe
   to the Messiah as a flower?

Malachi. I do.

Chorazim. Perhaps
   another metaphor were more apt. Suppose
   he's planted like an acorn in a jar,

which grows and spreads his roots and must become
a tree if he's to live. And then suppose
that we're the pottery that hems him in
and must be shattered when his swelling roots
reach out for earth.

Gennesareth. But obviously, Chorazim,
we cannot let self-interest affect us
in such a matter. Who values the clay pot
if by its breaking this eternal oak
is set in our soil to flourish forever?

Malachi. I value my clay pot.
And Herod values his, and Hanan his,
more than any oak or acorn.

Gennesareth. But think what you say!
You'd let them murder him and make no outcry—

Chorazim, Come, come, the word—
the word is strong—murder—

Gennesareth. Is it stronger than death?
For that's what they mean! Death!

Abbas. But think what you say,
Gennesareth! Suppose a Messiah comes
and the high priest does not welcome him, but finds
   him
worthy of death—are we not bound to believe
that he is worthy of death—that he is not
the true Messiah?

Gennesareth. If there were grave doubt, perhaps—
But any child or man who appeared and seemed
to be the Messiah, they would seek his death!
Whether he were doubtful or not!

Abbas. Would there not be doubt always?
What test have we for the true Messiah? None.
None generally accepted.

Gennesareth. Would you then—
if the Messiah were to stand before us—
if he came here—and revealed himself—would you—
report his presence to Hanan?

Chorazim. There is none
among us, my dear Gennesareth, who would care
to have it said, "The Messiah passed this way,
and spoke to you, and then went on, but you
of the Sanhedrin never knew him."

Gennesareth. Which means
if he came, you would betray him!

Abbas. Come, again,
the word again—the word is strong—betray—
why should we say betray? Let us say announce,
for that is our meaning. If the Messiah comes
I shall announce him gladly.

Chorazim. Yet he will not come—he will not come—
Be sure of that—the question will not arise.
The children of Israel are fools to hope for him
and the high priest and the king are fools to fear him—
for he will not come.

> [JESHUA *enters behind them.*]

Gennesareth. There are passages
as early as the pentateuch of Moses
that cannot be interpreted except
as the promise of his coming!

Chorazim. It is promised, yes.
And so we wait for it. Meanwhile the Romans

govern us as they like, and pick our pockets
with ease, because we're watching the gates of Heaven
for the coming of a god!

Malachi. My theory is—

Abbas. There's a child that listens.
Can it be that we are watched?

Gennesareth. This is Jeshua,
the son of my cousin Joseph of Nazareth,
who stays with me during Passover at my house.
[*To Jeshua*]
How did you come here?

Jeshua. I was walking here among the columns,
and thought I was alone till I heard your voices—
You will forgive me?

Malachi.

[*Continuing*]

My theory is that we
of this generation shall not see the Messiah
because he has come and gone. Two centuries
have passed since Judas Maccabaeus marched
to Jerusalem, expelling the foreign legions
that had conquered us. Could not our Maccabaeus
have been the Messiah? He fulfilled the conditions.
I think he was the Messiah, and that we
shall see no other.

Jeshua. But—Judas Maccabaeus
could not have been the Messiah!

Chorazim. No?—then why not?
Your kinsman's son has opinions of his own.

Jeshua. I'm sorry. I spoke without thinking. I had forgotten—
this is the court of the Sanhedrin—

Gennesareth. It is indeed not fitting that a child
should interrupt us.

Jeshua. Yes, I know.
[*He turns to go.*]

Malachi. And yet I should like to know why your cousin's
son
should say so passionately that Maccabaeus
could not have been the Messiah. For myself,
I cannot see why not.

Gennesareth. Stay, Jeshua—
stay and answer.

Jeshua. But you can answer this.
You could all answer better than I.

Chorazim. No, truly,
we have no answer.

Jeshua. We know the works of men
can be undone. We know that Maccabaeus
once set us free, but we were conquered again.
If Maccabaeus had been sent of God
we should still be free, for the works of God
cannot be undone.

Abbas. It's a shrewd answer.

Chorazim. Yes.
Yes, he has a certain logic
which is not bad.

Abbas. He lives in Galilee.

Malachi. Let's not despise the country. As you know
it's the shepherd boys come fresh from off the hills
who prosper in Jerusalem.

You learned this from your father, Jeshua,
or was it yours?

Jeshua. I've learned many things, from him,
but, I think not this. Isn't it a plain meaning?
It came to me—if the Messiah stood on earth,
alone, and found himself a man, expecting
no help from God, he could not have much hope.
He could have no hope at all.

Chorazim. I don't follow you.
You're too abstruse for me.

Jeshua. If it were given
to you to be the Messiah, and you stood
here in this room, and looked out over the earth,
and saw our poverty of men and things,
and knew that we were a pathway for the empires
that lie to east and west—would you have courage
even to begin?

Chorazim. But I am not the Messiah.

Jeshua. If he were a man, and without the help of God,
he would be much like you.

Chorazim.
   [*Smiling*]
Ah, a shrewd thrust!
The country boy strikes home! Take him off, someone,
because he bites and scratches!

Malachi. Well, here's a question
which has puzzled the wise men time out of mind—
When the Messiah comes will he descend
from heaven or be born, a man among men,
here on our earth?

Jeshua. He will be born among men.

Abbas.
   [*Smiling*]
   You see! He knows!

Malachi. Now you must have some reason—
   some weighty reason for this answer?

Jeshua. Yes.
   I have a reason.

Malachi. Give it, sir. We await you.

Jeshua. It's written that he's to come of the line of David,
   and David was a man.

Malachi. A casuist—
   [*He throws up his hands in mock despair.*]
   an absolutist and a casuist—
   I must admit that David was a man,
   and according to the prophet the Messiah
   will come of the line of David. Some country priest
   has worked these riddles out, brooding alone
   over his crust of shew-bread and the Torah,
   and schooled the boy in his answers.

Abbas. But now I think
   you've stepped into difficulties, Jeshua.
   The work of Maccabaeus was undone,
   you say, and therefore he was only a man,
   and therefore not the Messiah. But you also say
   the Messiah will be a man.

Jeshua. With the help of God.
   A man with the help of God.

Abbas. Is that so different?

Jeshua. Isn't it all the difference in the world?

Abbas. Yes, if a man were ever sure he had it—
it might be.

Jeshua. But a man would know if he had it.

Abbas. You think he would?

Jeshua. If God should speak to a man
the man would know.

Chorazim. I think when you grow up
you'll be among us here in the Sanhedrin—
But answer one last question:
How will you know the Messiah when he comes?

Malachi. Yes, how shall we know him?
Answer that, Jeshua.

Jeshua. By his victories.
By his great victories.
And by the immortal army from the sky
that fights beneath his banner.

Abbas. Oh, God will send an army!

Jeshua. He must.

Malachi. Is there any prophecy
regarding such an army?

Jeshua. No, there is none.
But could our little handful of tribes
win against Rome unless God sent us help
out of his Heaven? If there's to be a Messiah
God must help him!

Chorazim. Meanwhile, we've wandered far
from our last question: How shall we know the Messiah

when he appears? Instead of your vague answer
were it not better to put those facts together
which the prophecies reveal? It's true, as you say,
he's to come of the line of David. His birthplace, too,
has been predicted. No doubt you know it?

Jeshua. No.

Chorazim. You cannot name his birthplace?

Jeshua. No.

Malachi. There are gaps,
my scholar, in your erudition. The place
is named in a passage which you must have studied—
the fourth chapter of Micah. Let me quote it for you:
"But thou, town of Bethlehem,
though thou be little among the thousands of Judah,
yet out of thee shall come forth, Bethlehem Ephrata,
him who is to be the ruler of Israel."
Do you know these words?

Jeshua. No, this is new to me.
For I have studied all the other prophets
except only Micah.
   [*The music of a chant is heard from a distance.*]

Abbas. The ritual has begun,
and we shall be expected.

Chorazim.
   [*To* GENNESARETH]
Yes, we must go.
But bring your kinsman up to Jerusalem
when he's of an age to come.

Malachi. Yes, bring him when he's older, Gennesareth.
   [ABBAS *and* MALACHI *go out.*]

Gennesareth. Would you care to be one of us, Jeshua, when you are older?

Jeshua. To be with you here? Yes, and yet—
if God dwells here, should one not feel his presence
even in passing by?

Gennesareth. You haven't felt it
here in the Temple?

Jeshua.
   [*With self-reproach*]
   No.

Chorazim. Not in this room?

Jeshua. No. Least of all here in this room. But I
shall walk on further—and if I don't find it—then
I shall know the lack is in me, and not in the Temple,
for it is God's house.

CURTAIN

Act Two

Scene II

SCENE ♪ ♪ Before the Temple at Jerusalem. It is toward evening but the court and the steps are still busy with activities associated with the Passover.

The GREEK WOMAN is selling jewelry, and her neck and arms are loaded with bangles. The DOVE WOMAN is offering doves to passers-by, two MONEY-CHANGERS have set up shop on the steps, a MATZOH-SELLER is seated on a step, and a FRUIT-SELLER has spread his wares for sale. A PHARISEE stands behind them in silent prayer.

JESSE, REBA, ZEBULON, SHADRACH and CASSIA enter and stand in a group below the Temple steps.

Dove Woman. Buy my pigeons and doves!
Buy my white doves!

Greek Woman. Bangles, earrings and bracelets!

Fruit-Seller. Three sestercia a dozen, if you please!
Dates and figs from Syria!

Matzoh-Seller. Shew bread for the festival!
Shew bread!

1st Money-Changer. I can exchange into Greek or Roman
coinage
at the lowest rates. Copper, silver or gold
in the standard denarius of Rome, the drachma
of Athens, or for those who travel abroad,
the Egyptian obol. Farthings, mites, sestercia,
the Augustan aureus of soft gold, to be handled
lightly, lest you wear it down—

2nd Money-Changer. My charge
is definite and unvaried. One per cent

of all amounts above one aureus,
and below that, two per cent. My competitor
deducts an indefinite and exorbitant fee
which you feel though you do not see it!

1st Money-Changer. If you are wise
you will disbelieve the slanderous attack
of my associate at the next table, a man
of criminal record, the son of an Arab pirate
and a Phoenician strumpet, whose practice it is
to extract full fifty per cent of all he touches
and swear that he took but one!

2d Money-Changer. To his other virtues
the brigand on my right adds a practical knowledge
of sleight-of-hand, which enables him to delude you
with copper for gold, and deceive you as to your change.
Watch him carefully, I desire you.

Jesse. Why should we part with our shekels?
The shekels are good money!

The Greek Woman. Gold and silver ornaments from
Tyre!
Carved ivory combs from Asia! At no price!
For whatever you will pay!

[*Holding a bracelet out to* Cassia.]

This is Persian gold!

Cassia. Shadrach, I want a bangle.

Shadrach. Let me see.

Cassia. This.

Shadrach. But that's a cheap gaudy bangle. You wouldn't
want

a cheap, gaudy one like that.

Cassia. Yes. Yes, I would.

Shadrach. You don't need to be hung around with gew-
gaws;
You're still pretty without them.

Cassia. I know how it is.
When you're young you're handsome enough without
jewels—
and when you're old nobody will buy them for you.

Shadrach. I think the Pharisee's about to pray.
He's flapping his wings. Watch! Look!

The Pharisee. Oh God of Ezekiel,
look down upon these subtle and michievous men
who parley over money even in thy courts
and bring in dancing women for wives!

[JESHUA *enters. The vendors call out simultaneously.*]

Dove Woman. Buy my pigeons and doves!
Buy my white doves!

Greek Woman. Bangles, earrings and bracelets!

Fruit-Seller. Three sestercia a dozen, if you please!
Dates and figs from Syria!

Matzoh-Seller. Shew bread for the festival!

1st Money-Changer. I can exchange into Greek or Roman
coinage—

2d Money-Changer. My charge
is definite and unvaried—

The Pharisee.
[*Silencing them*]

Oh Jahveh,
when thou shalt make a desolation of cities,
when thou shalt come suddenly upon the men who
    dance
and the women who make music,
in that day spare me, who have kept myself perfect
and have not gone about to become unclean!

[MARIUS, *the soldier, enters.*]

Marius. The Tetrarch Herod
has ordered a distribution of alms!
On the first day of Passover in each year
the Tetrarch distributes silver! Today His Highness
is personally at the temple, to assure
that there is no injustice! To the court of the Gentiles
and take your place in the line!

[*The* MATZOH-SELLER *rises, picks up her basket and exits,
followed by the* GREEK WOMAN, *the* FRUIT-SELLER *with his
basket, and the* DOVE WOMAN *with her cages. The* MONEY-
CHANGERS *pick up their tables and follow, with the* PHARISEE
behind them and, after him, MARIUS.]

Shadrach. It looks as if business
was not so good, the way they abandon it.

Zebulon. Does he indeed give silver?

Jesse. Yes. No doubt Herod learned
this trick from Caesar, a giving of public money
to make all men his servants.

Shadrach.

[*Doubtful*]

And yet it is silver;
it's a day's wage. Will I go any more quickly
to the eternal grinding machine because
I took silver from Herod? I think not.

Reba. I think, since it's not an hour for prayer
and nothing is lost in duty or sacrifice,
we may accept the money.

Jesse. Why, let us take it then.
[SHADRACH, CASSIA *and* ZEBULON *go out.*]

Perhaps I speak for an older and sterner time
when the patriarchs taught a distrust of the gifts of
rulers.

[*He and* REBA *follow the others.* JESHUA *is left alone on
the stage, looking after them.* MIRIAM *enters.*]

Miriam. Joseph, he's here.
[JOSEPH *enters.*]

Jeshua. Father, there are money-changers here in the
Temple—
and Herod gives silver here.

Joseph. Yes, Jeshua.
But it should not be so—and was not when I was a
child.
There was no buying or selling licensed then
within the Temple enclosure.

Miriam. We were frightened, Jeshua,
and came to find you.

Jeshua. Mother, something so strange has happened.
I was in the court of the Sanhedrin
and they spoke of a prophecy I've never heard.
Father—why have we never studied Micah?
Why have I never heard of the prophecy
concerning Bethlehem?

Joseph. Will you let me tell you
a little later? It goes back so far

into many things that have happened. Many times
I've tried to think of how to tell you. Still—
I'm not sure.
And whatever I said to you—
might mislead. Might mislead you—and ourselves—
might fix our thinking. So that we quite believed
something we only guess. Perhaps this much
I can say now. When you were but a babe
and the first Herod still lived, I had a dream
warning that we must leave the realm of Herod
and carry you secretly to Egypt. Now,
we had no way of knowing whether my dream
was merely a dream—or a dream sent of God.
There is no proof of such things. But we were afraid,
and obeyed it, and went to Egypt. Then it came true—
for Herod killed all the children.

Jeshua. Yes. That I knew.

Joseph. But that was not all. When Herod died in this
    blood
and Herod's sons became governors of his kingdom,
we made our way back from Egypt—and again a dream
warned me against the province of Judea,
and we kept on north, to settle in Galilee
under Herod Antipas. And now we must question,
were we led wisely, was this last dream a delusion—?
Because so far there's no answer.

Jeshua. Only we've been safe.

Joseph. Yes. Safe until we came to the city gates.
    Then—while we waited—the robber came from the des-
    ert to take you through.

Miriam. And that, in a way, was an answer.

Joseph. Or may have been.

Jeshua. I must tell you—in one night
two or three years ago, when I'd been ill,
I felt you bending over me with a light
when I was half asleep—and heard mother saying:
"It's as if there were an ushering of wings
when I come to bring him water—and then a shadowing
of wings overhead, when I shield him from the sun—"
Do you remember, Mother, what you said?

Miriam. Yes, the whole air seemed troubled in the room,
as if I were never ministering alone,
but with bright companions.

Joseph. You're a child, Jeshua,
but you see how we've been troubled. From the beginning
our race has always held that there would come
a Messiah of our own, to release all Israel
and destroy those who oppress us. Now we're oppressed
as we were in former times, and we hear all about us
the whisper, and the cry, and the prophecy, too—
"The Messiah, the Messiah! . . ." How are we to know
that we have not dreamed because of our desire?
It's not fair to lay the burden of this question on a
child—
for it's only a question. It may not be true—
but if you were he—in such case would it be fair
to keep it from you?

Jeshua. But, Father, would this be a burden?
Mother, would this be a burden? You speak so strange-
ly!
The Messiah is the Promised One, the Anointed
who comes to us with an army, with the bright sword

of justice, to war on evil, and make an end
of weeping in Israel! I have nothing in me
to make me this prince who is promised.—You know me
    well,
and I am only your Jeshua, who reads
too much, and goes about too much in dreams
of the old heroes.—But if the day has come now
for our Messiah—whether it light on me
or another child—is it anything to be feared?
Let us say it is not for me—but it is our hope,
the coming of the Messiah! Isn't it, Mother?

Miriam. Yes, Jeshua.

Joseph. And yet our race—
    our dark, fierce, wistful race will not see the earth
    as the earth is. We live in a doubtful legend,
    and tell ourselves these tales—

Jeshua. The Messiah's promised
    even in the wisdom of Solomon, the latest
    of all the wise books we have!

Joseph. Yes, I know that.
    The sun's dropped below the wall. It's time to go.
    We have half an hour.

Jeshua. Could I sit here on the step—
    just a few minutes?

Joseph. We dare not leave you, Jeshua.

Miriam. No, we dare not.
    We must take you with us.

Joseph. I think it's best that you should come with us now
    and never go out alone till we return
    to our house in Nazareth.

Jeshua. May I not stay in the Temple?
There was something I wished to find here. And haven't
found.
If I could sit here alone—

Miriam. We took no care
at the gates—yet he was cared for. If this is a wish
and from his heart—it may be wrong to take thought—
we may lead him into danger.

Joseph. Then we'll leave you, Jeshua.
But come before it's dark.

Jeshua. Yes, Father.

> [JOSEPH *and* MIRIAM *go out.* JESHUA *sits on the step with
> his head in his hand.* FLACCUS, FESTUS *and* MARIUS *enter and
> cross the stage.* MARIUS *pauses and looks back at* JESHUA,
> *then the* SOLDIERS *go out.* ISHMAEL *enters with a dagger in
> his hand. When he sees that* MARIUS *has gone, he replaces
> the dagger in his belt.*]

Ishmael. Jeshua!

> [JESHUA *rises.*]

You know who I am?

Jeshua. The prophet from the desert.
The prophet Ishmael.

Ishmael. Not the robber Ishmael?

Jeshua. Are you not a prophet?

Ishmael. I am sent of God.
Whether a prophet or some lesser tongue
I shall not know. But God has given me words
and my message is to you. Listen carefully
for we have little time.

Jeshua. My father and mother have asked me to come
  home
before the service. I fear I shall be late.
Could you come with me?

Ishmael. No, I must say it now,
and you must hear it now. Though you be late.
This is the culmination of my life,
and for you it means the beginning. You may stay now
or go—to join the others forever.

Jeshua. Then
if I go, I could not see you tomorrow?

Ishmael. No.
I shall not speak tomorrow. Only tonight
is illumined with the crossing of two stars,
one dying and one born.

Jeshua. Is it good or evil
you bring me?

Ishmael. When you are older you will know good from
  evil.
Tonight you will not know.

Jeshua. Let me go home.

Ishmael. Yes.

  [JESHUA *starts to go out, then stops and turns.*]

Jeshua. I must stay to listen.
I do trust you. You took me through the gates
and watched over us in the desert.

Ishmael. When I spoke
and knew you in the desert, did you know then
why I watched over you?

Jeshua. No.

Ishmael. Do you know now?
   [JESHUA *is silent.*]
   Because I saw
   The Messiah in your eyes, and, taking your silver,
   felt the immortal substance in your hand,
   burning my clay. Are you not the Messiah?

Jeshua. I have dreamed I was the Messiah.

Ishmael. In the night—
   or a waking dream?

Jeshua. First it came in the night—
   then I remembered the dream, and called it back
   to see the beauty of fiery images
   and the men who came from the sky.

Ishmael. Tell me your dream.

Jeshua. I have never told it.

Ishmael. No, but tell it to me,
   for my message has to do with it.

Jeshua. I walked
   among the cedars over Lebanon,
   and said to myself the words of the Unknown Prophet
   who has written in Isaiah—"Awake, awake,
   put on strength, O arm of the Lord! Awake,
   as in the ancient days, in the generations
   of olden time!" And, as I said these words,
   I heard a distant singing, and a little door
   was opened in the sky, high overhead
   many roods above me. Out of this small door
   came shining warriors clad in steel and silver

who marched out into the clouds. Then a voice said,
"Go up to them." And I said, "I cannot go,
because they walk on cloud," but the voice said, "Try,"
and so I essayed a step, and the moving air
had set itself like stone beneath my feet,
so that I could climb. Then I went up the cloud
among the army, and took the sword that hung
above the door in the sky, and we came together
down the steps of air. The Romans had drawn up
across the Phoenician plain, toward the great sea,
but when they saw that we walked above the sunrise
they sent out an embassy. This came to me,
and I said, "Send out the evil men." They sent
the men from galleys and prisons, but all these
I turned back to them, and said again, "Send out
the evil men," This time they sent the beggars
and the panders from the streets, but I turned them
    back,
and said, "This one last time I ask it of you—
send out the evil men!" Then they sent their kings
and the Emperor Augustus, and the tetrarchs,
and the men who are set over at tasks and taxing,
with the officers beneath them. And I came here
to the holy city, to make it my capital,
and rule wisely and justly. This was my dream—
and now I've told it.

   [*There is a pause.*]

Ishmael. Child, child, how can I tell you?
  I haven't wept since the death of Judah, but now
  I find myself weeping.

Jeshua. Was this an evil dream?

Ishmael. Not evil, but mistaken. If you wish to go

you should go now—go back to Nazareth
and root yourself there among poor villagers
who are happy with what they have.

Jeshua. Why should I go?

Ishmael. Because there's no turning back once I've spoken
  to you.
  Because it is my mission to fill your soul
  with a torment that will become an exaltation—
  because it is your mission to torment
  the earth, and exalt it.
  But tonight you will look with a child's eyes into dark-
    ness
  and not see beyond.

Jeshua. How was my dream mistaken?

Ishmael. It is true the Messiah
  will stand before the officers and the people
  and say, "Send out the evil men!" But he
  will make this demand alone. There will come no army
  out of the sky to help. He will have few friends
  and they will not understand him. He will have wis-
    dom
  and will cry out wisdom to all men in the streets
  but they will not hear.
  The words that come from his mouth
  will scatter on barrens and in meagre places.
  He will be defeated. He will cause laughter
  and be set aside.

Jeshua. But now I think you speak evil.
  You have not read the prophets. I will not believe you.
  The Messiah will win victories! You know
  the Messiah must conquer!

Ishmael. Yes, after a thousand years—
or ten thousand.

Jeshua. How could it be he conquered
after a thousand years?

Ishmael. Or after ten thousand.
After these years the memory of his face
and the words he said, and his unearned affliction
will move among men—will catch and move among
   them
like fire—and they will turn and follow him—
seeing evil where he saw it.

Jeshua. How can you know this?
This is a dream like mine.

Ishmael. I once believed
that he would win his victories in the field,
our Jewish Messiah. But, living in the hills,
with little to eat, and no solace for the mind
save the reading of God's word,
I set myself to study what was said
concerning the Messiah—and I found
that none had understood. You quote to me
the Unknown Prophet in Isaiah. Listen!
these words are his:
"He was oppressed and he was afflicted,
yet he opened not his mouth:
he is brought as a lamb to the slaughter
and, as a sheep before her shearers is dumb,
so he opened not his mouth.
He was taken from prison and from judgment,
and who shall declare his generation?
For he was cut off out of the land of the living,

for the transgression of my people was he stricken."
Do you know what this means?

Jeshua. It seems to me a dark saying.

Ishmael. It means that the guiltless
must suffer for the guilty, that the good are those
who live their lives for others—that those who are evil,
those who are base, are lifted up and vouchsafed
redemption through this suffering.

Jeshua. But what has this
to do with the Messiah? Or with me?
The Messiah is sent to conquer the Romans!

Ishmael. Yes—
but not as you understand the meaning of conquest,
The Messiah is sent to hunt out wisdom and truth,
to speak this wisdom and truth in love to those
who need his love, and in bitterness to those
who have earned bitterness. And in the end
for this love and bitterness with which he speaks
he will become a symbol of those who are guiltless—
and those who are guilty, seeing in him this symbol,
will turn and destroy him. He will suffer for them
and conquer them in their hearts.

Jeshua. The Messiah is not to suffer. He is not sent
to suffer for others. I have never heard this said
by my father or in the temple.

Ishmael. Remember the prophets—
and listen again. "Yet it hath pleased the Lord
to bruise him.—He hath put him to grief.
Because he hath poured out his soul unto death;
and he was numbered with the transgressors,
and he bore the sin of many." You have read this?

Jeshua. Yes.

Ishmael. Has it any meaning?

Jeshua. Yes, it is true. I have read
these things, and wondered. Yet if this is the Messiah
the elders are wrong—and my father.

Ishmael. Yes, they are wrong.

Jeshua. Some of the words seem to say that he must die—
that the Messiah must die.

Ishmael. Even this is true. He will die early;
a hateful and intolerable death,
and nails will be through his hands.

Jeshua. Who has sent you to me?

Ishmael. Who it is that orders the wheeling of the nights
and hung your star on the mountain. Do you believe
me?
Do you believe that I am come from God
and speak his word?

Jeshua. Yes. If I must.—
When must he die?

Ishmael. When he has spoken his wisdom, and the earth
is roused up against him.

Jeshua. Could he not keep silent?

Ishmael. No.
What he has to say he must say, what he has
to do he must do.

Jeshua. There will be torture used
before he dies?

Ishmael. Yes.

Jeshua. No, I cannot! I cannot!
  I have never borne pain! I cannot bear pain!
  And I'm afraid of death!
  I cannot face death! I say this is not for me—
  to be this Messiah!

Ishmael. Yet you will bear it!

Jeshua. No!

Ishmael. But if you were frightened—if you were afraid—
  afraid of Herod and of Herod's men—
  and ran—then Herod would win—then you'd die quick-
     ly
  and all men would die with you.

Jeshua. If I were afraid?

Ishmael. Yes, if you were afraid.—You will go your way
  and be a child and forget. Yet in your mind
  what we have said will become a leaven that works
  in all you are and do.

Jeshua. Why did I trust you?
  It's grown dark, and you're a stranger! I must go home!

Ishmael. I've given you all I have. I'm weary now
  and empty. Go if you wish.

Jeshua. If there were only someone I could ask!
  Someone who could give an answer!

Ishmael. Go into the Temple and pray
  for your old dream. If your God will give it back
  then you may have it still.

Jeshua. Yes, I will pray.

  [*He goes out.* MARIUS *enters opposite.*]

Marius. I heard your conversation with the boy—
  the boy who was your son when I first saw you
  at the gates of the city. I heard what you said to him.
  What kind of madman are you?

Ishmael. God knows how mad I am—
  and spent and weak and empty—

Marius. Something you said
  to this boy had a kind of meaning for me;
  I've been set here to watch the Temple
  and guard against a Messiah. What this is
  I never have quite known. But now it seems
  you feel quite certain what the Messiah is,
  and this lad is he. Is that true?

Ishmael.

  [*Looks away, then back before he speaks.*]

  Yes, it is true.
  I looked to my God for an answer, and within
  I heard his voice: "Speak to the soldier boldly,
  and say, 'This is the Messiah.'"

Marius. I'm grateful to you,
  and to your God, who makes things simple and clear
  even to men-at-arms,

  [*He crosses toward the Temple.* ISHMAEL *takes out his dagger.* MARIUS *turns.*]

  for I should hesitate indeed to strike down
  a child without good warrant. But I think your word
  is quite sufficient.

  [*He draws his sword and goes toward the inner Temple.* ISHMAEL *runs lightly after* MARIUS *and leaps to his back. A knife flashes and* MARIUS *is wounded, but turns and strikes down* ISHMAEL *with his sword.* ISHMAEL *lies where*

he falls; MARIUS *has sunk to one knee but rises and stag-
gers out.*]

Marius. Flaccus! Festus! I'm wounded!
[*As he goes*]

Help, Flaccus—the beggar—help!
[*He crashes to the flag-stones offstage.* JESHUA *comes out of
the Temple, sees* ISHMAEL *and runs to him.*]

Jeshua. Ishmael! Ishmael! You're hurt!
What is it? There's a trail of blood out toward the
court!

Ishmael. Run back, Jeshua! Run back into the Temple!
The soldiers will come and find you here!

Jeshua. But, Ishmael,
I dare not run away! I dare not be frightened!

Ishmael. Quick, quick!

Jeshua. You warned me not to run away,
and you spoke for God!
[*He holds* ISHMAEL'S *head on his arm.*]

Festus.
[*Outside*]
The beggar had a knife!

Flaccus.
[*Outside*]
There's no life in him!

Festus.
[*Entering*]
That's the fellow, there!

Flaccus.
> [*Enters*]
> There's a child with him!

Festus. Put the spawn out of the way—
the dirty beggar and all his generation!

Flaccus. Make him run then.

Festus. Yes, make him run, that's best,
and cut him down as he runs.
> [*They come near* JESHUA.]
> Run! Run while you can!
> Do you want to die there on the stones?
> [JESHUA *rises and faces them.*]

Jeshua. Are you Herod's men?

Festus. Yes, we are Herod's men.

Jeshua. I went into the Temple
and prayed to God. I asked him whether Ishmael
was false or a true man. Then a voice spoke out loud
and said, "He is a messenger of my word.
Follow him and turn not back." I cannot run
from Herod's men, nor be frightened of them.
> [FESTUS *draws sword.*]

Festus. This is a clean, sharp sword! Do you want your
blood to
darken it?

Jeshua. No.

Festus. Then let me see you run
while you still can run!

Jeshua. But if I run
   from Herod or Herod's men, I shall die quickly,
   having displeased my God! I must stay and face you.

   [*There is an uncertain pause.*]

Flaccus. Put up your sword.
   You can't strike down a child who looks up at you.
   Let them alone. There's some necromancy
   with these Jewish gods and temples. And the beggar's
      dying.
   Let them alone.

Festus. Very well.

   [FESTUS *and* FLACCUS *go out.* JESHUA *sits and again pillows
   the old man's head on his arm.*]

CURTAIN

JOURNEY TO JERUSALEM

ACT THREE

Act Three

SCENE I

SCENE ᛒ ᛒ The roof of HEROD'S *palace.* HEROD *and* MIRA *are looking out over the city.*

Mira. For ten days now they have done no work. The walls
of our new palace stand as they stood then,
below the line of trees. Is it abandoned?
Is it never to be finished?

Herod. Why do you ask?

Mira. Because there's been no work done these ten days.

Herod. This is the time of year when all the Jews
go up to Jerusalem. I encouraged them
to go this year—for my purposes. But now
the work will be resumed. Before the end
of summer, you will have your apartments
overlooking the lake. For now the work
will proceed with a vengeance. There's been too much
talk
among the Jews, and too little done.
  [*The* SOOTHSAYER *enters.*]
Yes?

Soothsayer. The high priest, Hanan,
my lord, and a centurion, and with them
the scribe who sat at the gate.

Herod. Let them enter.

Mira. Then—
it's better if I leave you.

Herod. No, stay if you like.

[HANAN, *the* SCRIBE, *and the* CENTURION *enter*.]
With you I put aside all secrecy,
as with these officers.

Hanan. Good evening, my lord.

Herod. Good evening, my lord Hanan,
and to you, and you. You all know what I seek for.
Give me what evidence you have. I begin
at once, Lord Hanan, and begin with you.
Has the rumor of this presence passed your way?

Hanan. I have had no word.

Herod. You conveyed my message
to the scribes and priests?

Hanan. Yes. As you said it to me,
Lord Herod.

Herod. There came no answer—of any sort—
no cryptic message, wrapped in words, which I
might understand if I heard it?

Hanan. Not a whisper
from all the Temple.

Herod. You were thorough? There has been
no miracle, no sudden apparition
to those that tend the altar, no power of faith
beyond what's human; no wisdom in the Temple
or among the men of the Sanhedrin beyond
what's usual there?

Hanan. I should have heard of it,
of that I'm certain.

Herod. Then you, sir—taking the census,

some unexpected presence at the gates
disturbed you for a moment—on some day
which may come back to you now I mention it.—
Some child with a strange wisdom on his face
that caused your hair to rise, just for a moment,
and then was forgotten?

Scribe. Your Highness, I hesitate
to speak of this, lest I seem negligent,
but there is one face, out of those that passed the gates,
which haunts me in the night.

Herod. The face of a child?

Scribe. Yes, of a child.

Herod. Was he of the age and city
which have been specified?

Scribe. No, he was not.

Herod. But bring him to me.

Scribe. My lord, although his name
is written in the records, he was born
and lives still on the foot-hills of Mount Nebo—
the son of a bandit or a wild tribesman. This
is desert country, full of desperate men,
impossible to search.

Herod. Yet we will search there!
We will search the plains of Nebo thoroughly.
I give you this task.

Scribe.
   [*Bowing and stepping back*]
   Yes, my lord.

Herod. Centurion!

Centurion. Yes.

Herod. How did it come that a trusted man was killed
in the Temple court—a man I myself had set
to guard against the Messiah?

Centurion. He was struck down
by a wild man from the desert—and the wild man
was killed in his turn. This would seem to end the matter.

Herod. Was there a child
about the Temple, or near it, at the time?

Centurion. Nothing was said of a child.

Herod. Everywhere he eludes me,
and he does elude me, for he was there.
His hand was in this. Can it be, I wonder
that he has left our kingdom?

Soothsayer. My lord, look where
his star still hangs on the Galilean night,
and out-burns Jupiter, and dims great Mars
along the west. He is here.

Herod. Try this stratagem,
Centurion—try this! My wife has asked
why the work's slow on our palace. From now on
the work will go rapidly. Use what force you need;
drive them, listen to no excuses; let
them understand that they are slaves, incite
our Galilee to rebellion if you can.
Then out of this we'll get our palace done,
and out of this, if there should be rebellion,
and it should find a leader, there's our man—

he'll be the one we seek. Do you understand?

Centurion. Make them desperate, and look for a leader.

Herod. Yes.
  And now you may go. Go all of you except
  Mira, my wife.
    [*The* SCRIBE, *the* CENTURION, *the* SOOTHSAYER, *and* HANAN *go
    out.*]

Mira. We may get our palace done,
  and for that I thank you. But let the Messiah go,
  for he has escaped you!

Herod. Escaped me? It's in my star—
  that I shall destroy the Messiah! It's in his star
  that I shall destroy him! Though he escape me now,
  as he may—though he escape me for years, yet soon
  or late, I shall be his death.
  Yet sometimes it seems
  that I seek the impalpable, try to put my finger
  on that which walks the streets and is not seen,
  on that which pierces to the heart, yet leaves
  no wound or scar. Suppose the Messiah came
  like the voice of a bird, suppose he came like dawn
  across the earth? What man has turned back the morn-
    ing?
  What king has taken the measure of the wind?

CURTAIN

ACT THREE

Scene II

SCENE ❧ ❧ Joseph's house at Nazareth. It is morning. Miriam has risen from her work to welcome Jesse and Zebulon, who enter.

Jesse. Forgive us, Miriam.
Joseph has asked us to go in. The Centurion
wishes to see us all together.
[Shadrach *comes down the steps.*]

Miriam. Surely.
Come in. Come in, Shadrach.

Shadrach. I wish I had
the faith I had formerly in Ecclesiastes;
He says, "He that diggeth a pit shall fall therein;
and whoso breaketh through a fence, a serpent
shall bite him." And yet for a good many years now,
    men
have been digging holes for others, and burying
the others in them, without falling in. And men
go right on smashing fences, and meet no snakes—
or no more than honest men. My Ecclesiastes
was an optimist, after all.
[Jeshua *enters, carrying a scroll.*]

Zebulon. We stopped
to speak to Jeshua, because the Centurion asked
for Joseph's helper.

Miriam. Yes.

Jesse. We heard one bit
of news at the market. There's a fish found living
in the Dead Sea. Not very large, and not

very edible—but a fish, and alive.

Shadrach. More than one?

Zebulon. Whole families of them. Up at the northern end
where the fresh water comes in.

Shadrach. And in Galilee
there are still Jews found living. Maybe not
very numerous, or edible, but still
existing among the back streets and high farms
where there aren't too many Romans.

Joseph.

[*Speaking to the* CENTURION *as he comes down the steps*]
Come in, sir.
You'll find us all under one roof, and waiting for you.
Whatever you have to say to us can be said
without a waste of voice.

[*The* CENTURION *enters after* JOSEPH.]

Centurion. As you remember I was easy with you
when I was here last. Things have changed a little.
I can't make you the same offer. You'll come to work,
and you'll take your chance as to who's the overseer
and what you'll get to do.

[*To* JOSEPH]
You once said to me,
there are no slaves in Galilee.—That's changed.
That's different now. There are slaves.—I want five men
from this house at the palace this morning.
If you want to know
what's different now—I'll tell you. You're trouble-
	makers.
You've been seen in company we don't like—
men from the desert—and prophets that go about

inciting to revolt. There was a beggar
around this house before you left, and another
was seen with you on the road to Jerusalem.
Judah's men probably—both of them. You know
when you're wanted—and where. You'll come.

[*He turns, goes up steps and out.*]

Zebulon. The voice of Caesar.

Joseph. Yes,
and of Herod.—I tried to put it from my mind
while we were away. But under the happiness
of our journey, under the ritual of the Temple
and under our holy songs, this undertone
was heard incessantly: We must return
to face the Centurion.

Shadrach. How can we serve them
and keep our faith—even a shred of faith?

Jesse. But disobedience to a Roman edict
means death for all of us.

Shadrach. If we had a leader!

Joseph. If we had a leader, such as Judah was—
yet even if we had a leader—even then
our revolution would end as Judah's ended—
in death for many, and life on the hills for many—
and nothing gained.

Shadrach. A leader like Moses then,
who could take us out of this into something better—
something with a hope in it!

Joseph. I've heard it said
there are no more promised lands.

Jesse. But easy, Shadrach—
this is a matter of bones in a cemetery.
Bones are not sacred.

Shadrach. To them it means desecration!
They spit on our lips and our altars! And our God
is up for sale in Jerusalem! We saw it,
and this is all part of it!

Joseph. If the men will come with me
we can talk this over better among ourselves.
[SHADRACH, ZEBULON, JESSE *and* JOSEPH *go toward the portal.*
JESHUA *rises.*]
No, not you, Jeshua.
[*The men go out.*]

Miriam. You should take your eyes
from your book sometimes, my Jeshua. You read
as if there were great haste.

Jeshua. Do I, Mother?

Miriam. Yes.
As if you were fevered, and only more and more reading
would quench your thirst.

Jeshua. It is like that.

Miriam. What water
is it you seek, my son, reading your eyes out
early in the morning, and then into the night,
till the last light's gone?
[*He is silent.*]
What was it happened
the night you were late at the Temple?

Jeshua. Oh, mother, tell me—

is it true—or did I imagine it—
that I stayed all night with the prophet before he died
in the court of the Temple—and you found me there
in the early morning?

Miriam. We came in the early morning
and found you there.

Jeshua. Then it may all be true—
it may be true—even in this bright daylight!
Oh, Mother,
is it so sure—is it certain, Mother, that I—
am this one—who is chosen?

Miriam. Your father's not sure.

Jeshua. But you—you, Mother—or was it my father alone
who dreamed? Did nothing come to you?

Miriam. No dream.

Jeshua. Then was it all his wishing, as he had feared,
his own desire?

Miriam. Could you believe so, Jeshua?

Jeshua. I could wish to believe so.

Miriam. When you are older
you shall know all my heart in all these things,
when you're only a little older.

Jeshua. Tell me your heart.
Say it now.

Miriam. Why, Jeshua?

Jeshua. Because it's part of my fever—
that I must hear it. Because I must know what I am

and what will come to me. In all this I read
in the holy books it's as if I set my lips
to Dead Sea water, so that I'm thirstier still—
and must know more!

Miriam. What do you read?

Jeshua. The prophecies.

Miriam. Concerning the Messiah?

Jeshua. Yes.

Miriam. If I
  could tell you now—

  [*She puts out her hand to* JESHUA. JESHUA *sits on floor at
  her feet.*]

  Mine was no dream, but a vision.
  I've never said this—
  perhaps I can't say it now. When a mother speaks
  to a son who is twelve years old, there's a veil woven
  between what she may know and he may hear—
  it's as it was when you tried to tell your dream—
  do you remember?

Jeshua. Yes.

Miriam. And now I find
  that I cannot speak. Only an angel came
  to me in a vision, saying when you were born
  your name was to be called Jeshua, and of your kingdom
  there was to be no end.
  This you may keep in your heart, as I have kept it
  till now in mine. You are indeed—you are He.
  Whatever has been prophesied for Him
  will be yours, will come to us—and we shall see it
  when you are grown a man.

Jeshua. Oh, mother, I know
  you wouldn't hurt me—

Miriam. Hurt you, Jeshua?
  But it was you who said in the outer court
  of the Temple, that this was not a burden—that it
  could mean only happiness.

Jeshua. Yes, I said it then.—
  When you spoke with the angel did you learn from him
  how the Messiah must die?

Miriam. I have never heard
  that he will die. There is to be no end
  to the Messiah's kingdom.

Jeshua. But he must die.
  This is what I heard from the robber prophet,
  from Ishmael, when he lay dying in the court,
  and I held his hand. The Messiah will not live
  to see his kingdom. He will be arraigned and tortured,
  and die under torture. He will find a teaching
  which can save men, but they will not follow it.
  They will despise him, will send soldiers to find him
  and set him before the judges. He will die
  to save others. This was said to me by the robber,
  and I couldn't believe him. But now I read the rolls
  day and night—read all the passages
  that have to do with his coming. And it's true
  if I'm chosen the Messiah then what it means
  is that I'm chosen out of all the children
  to be tortured for the others when the time comes
  for us to be men together. It's not a kingship—
  not to lead armies, not to die old, or in battle,
  but to be hurried to a sacrifice
  and die young, a criminal's death!

Miriam. He was evil, evil—
  this man from the desert!

Jeshua. I said he was evil! Yes,
  it seemed like madness to me! But all the books
  say what he said—it's there to be read by all
  who wish to read it!

Miriam. But it has no meaning!

Jeshua. Yes,
  Mother, it has a meaning. Its meaning is
  that the death of the innocent will work in the hearts
  of those who murder them, till the murderers
  are sorry, and have changed, and never again
  take life unjustly! It may mean more, may mean even
  that our race is chosen, our poor race of Israel,
  to suffer for other races, as the Messiah
  must suffer for our own.

Miriam. Where have you read this?

Jeshua. In all of them. That's why I've lain awake
  to read when light came into the sky at morning,
  and at night till my lamp went out. And they do say
    this.
  How we could all have missed it, and hoped so long
  for angels out of Heaven, I don't know—
  for it's plain there in the prophecies; there's to be
  no help come down from God. Our help must come
  from within, from our hearts, from those who are will-
    ing to die
  rather than accept injustice. And now you tell me
  your vision. And I know. I must somehow find
  the truth, according to my soul, and speak it,

and die for it—hoping somehow it will prevail
long after I'm dead.

Miriam. I will not believe this, Jeshua—

Jeshua. But I wish you would.
Then I wouldn't be alone. In all the world
there was only Ishmael knew this; and he died
for saying it to me. And now I must carry it.
Will you read the books?

Miriam. I'll read them if you like.
If it will help.

Jeshua. And then we can talk about them.

Miriam. Yes.

Jeshua. The book of Enoch says it clearly.

Miriam. I'll read the book of Enoch.

Jeshua. You'll read it first?

Miriam. Yes. First of all.—If this were what it means
to be the Messiah—to suffer and to die
for others—if it were not an honor—no,
but a dishonored death and misery—

Jeshua. Yes?

Miriam. Would you choose it then—?

Jeshua. If I should find
that I'm still chosen and still wanted when
I come to be a man, then it may be God
would help me. Maybe even if I came to you
you could help me then.

Miriam. I, Jeshua?

Jeshua. We shall be older.
 We shall both have learned by then.
 I must find my apron and the helper's tools.
   [JOSEPH, SHADRACH, JESSE *and* ZEBULON *enter.*]

Joseph. If we are to go
 we must go soon. And Jeshua should be ready.
 There were five called for.

Shadrach. Yet I still say what hope
 have we as a nation? Give us a little something
 to look forward to, and we can go on! But what is there,
 unless it's plain slavery?

Miriam. Is our Jeshua
 a workman among you?

Jesse. Yes.

Miriam. Could he speak to you
 as if he were a man?

Jesse. Yes, if he wishes.
 Do you wish to speak, Jeshua?

Jeshua. I have nothing
 of my own to say. But just as Shadrach asked
 what hope we have, the book of Enoch opened
 under my hand, to a part that I've read often.
 May I read it?

Shadrach. Yes, read it.

Jeshua. It's the last chapter.
 "A city is but the outer hull, or garment,
 of the faith which dwells within. Its palaces
 and walls that stand up nobly in the air
 and seem so tough and durable, are blown

↳ 105 ↰

into these shapes by the spirit which inhabits—
blown like a bubble, and will subside again
when the spirit is withdrawn. And what is true
of cities is true of kingdoms. For a cycle of years
they keep their faith, and this faith holds them steady
against the winds. But when they cease to believe
only a little while, the high roofs take rain,
and the walls sink to the moat. There was once a city
whose walls were destroyed by music blown against
    them,
but the walls of every city are raised up
by music, and are held foursquare in the sun
by a people's secret singing."

Shadrach. I must read the Scriptures.
    There are others beside Ecclesiastes.

Jeshua. Yes. Then he says:
    "The palace built by a king without a faith
    will not endure—but there are palaces
    not built by hands, and those cannot be torn down
    by the hands of kings."

Shadrach. It's true.
    The kings do lose in the end—and that's a hope,
    even for the people of Israel. But tell us then;
    Are we never to turn on the kings?
    Where is the line? How far can a man serve Herod?

Jeshua. Until he asks of you what belongs to God.
    [MIRIAM *rises and looks at* JOSEPH.]

Joseph. Until he asks of us what belongs to God.

Shadrach. What part of a man belongs to God?

Jeshua. His mind,
   his freedom, his freedom to find his way to God
   in his own way.

Shadrach.
   [*Turns to others.*]
   Well, shall we go?

Zebulon.
   [*Rising*]
   Why, yes,
   we can go now.
   [*He and* JESSE *go out.*]

Joseph. And you've not lost your faith?

Shadrach. Lost it? Lost my faith? I've just now found it.
   Just this moment found it.
   [*He goes out.*]

Joseph. So have I, I think. Yes, so have I.
   [*He follows the others.*]

Jeshua. I must go with them, Mother, I'm needed, too.

Miriam. Yes, Jeshua.
   [*She kisses his forehead.* JESHUA *goes out.*]

CURTAIN

7469